Aunt Ellen's
KNITTING
HANDBOOK
A Treasury of Techniques and Projects

by the Staff of THE WORKBASKET Magazine

Modern Handcraft, Inc.   Kansas City

ATTENTION: SCHOOLS AND BUSINESS FIRMS
Modern Handcraft books are available at quantity discounts for bulk purchases for educational, business or sales promotional use.

All inquiries should be addressed to Modern Handcraft, Inc.
4251 Pennsylvania, Kansas City, Missouri 64111

Printed in the United States of America

LIBRARY OF CONGRESS CATALOGING IN PUBLICATION DATA

Ellen, Aunt.
    Aunt Ellen's Knitting handbook.

    1. Knitting. I. Workbasket. II. Title.
III. Title: Knitting handbook.
TT820.A84   746.43'2   81-82242
ISBN 0-86675-326-5   AACR2

Contents

A Message from Aunt Ellen

Dear Reader:

Knitting is one of the oldest and most productive of the needlecrafts. This handbook was written to help you learn to knit or, if you already know how, to further your enjoyment of knitting.

Beginners will learn the secret of knitting: all the fancy designs are merely variations and combinations of the two basic stitches—knit stitch and purl stitch—both quickly learned.

If you already know how to knit, this book will serve you well as a source of interesting WORKBASKET projects, a refresher for popular pattern stitches, and a handy reference manual on body measurements. This simplified guide has been carefully organized with a complete table of contents to help you find what you want quickly and easily.

Happy Knitting!

Aunt Ellen

Aunt Ellen
The Workbasket Magazine

Knitting Needles And Accessories

There are various types of knitting needles available, each designed to serve a specific need or purpose. Once made of wood, bone and steel, American knitting needles today are made primarily of aluminum, plastic or nylon.

In America, knitting needle diameters are gauged in ascending order. That is, size 2 is larger than size 1. The following chart shows the most popular types and sizes of knitting needles and related accessories available.

INSTRUMENT	LENGTHS AVAILABLE	SIZES
Aluminum Knitting Needles		
Single Pointed	10"	0-15
	14"	0-15

Double Pointed	7"	0-8
	10"	1-8

Plastic Knitting Needles		
Single Pointed	10"	2-15
	14"	2-15
Single Pointed Jumbo (hollow)	14"	17, 18, 19, 35, 50

Double Pointed	7"	2-8
	10"	9-15

Circular Knitting Needles

Double Pointed—all steel,
or nylon with metal tips

LENGTHS AVAILABLE	SIZES
16″	0-10½
24″	0-10½
29″	0-15
36″	5-15

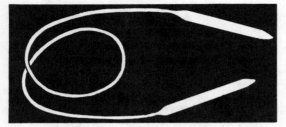

Jumper Knitting Needles

Single Pointed—all nylon or with
plastic or metal tips

18″	2-15

Point Protectors

To guard points from harm and to hold
stitches on needles when they are not being
worked

Various sizes

Stitch Holders (Safety Pin Style)

To store stitches in proper shapes and place
temporarily until needed

Various sizes

Cable Stitch Holders

To hold temporarily a few loops until needed
to complete cable stitching

Various sizes

Yarn Needle
For sewing knitted pieces together

Yarn End Weaver
For working loose ends of yarn back through a knitted piece to hide them, thus giving a finished appearance

Yarn Bobbin
For holding different colors of yarn being used in multi-colored work; sized for standard or bulky yarns

2½″, 5″

Stitch Count Markers
For holding points of decrease, increase and other necessary reminders

Crochet Hooks
For picking up dropped stitches and other catch-yarn-and-draw-through functions, such as closing seams

Various lengths
Various sizes

Stitch Gauge
For checking the number of stitches to the inch horizontally, and the number of rows to the inch vertically. (See back cover)

In addition to what your project calls for, you will also want to have handy such items as embroidery scissors, a tape measure, a note pad and pencil or a pegboard for keeping stitch count. Be in no hurry to acquire knitting implements. Get only those required for your project as there are some things shown here that you may never need.

Choosing The Right Yarn

Selecting the right yarn for a knitting project will have a bearing on its beauty and serviceability. Yarn is made up of loosely twisted natural fibers or cleverly fashioned man-made filaments. Generally, it is soft, fuzzy, pliable and elastic. It is helpful to know what properties to look for in quality yarn.

First and foremost, use the yarn specified in the instructions if you want the same results the directions promise. Any changes from the recommended yarn could make a decided difference in the finished product.

Yarns are dyed in lots or batches and no two lots are precisely the same shade. Thus, manufacturers print the dye lot number on the labels. When buying yarn, always get all you'll need for a project with the same dye lot number to be sure your finished article will be uniform in color throughout and won't be streaked by different shades.

Think in terms of how the item will be used in determining whether the colors need to be "color fast" (non-fading after repeated washings) or "light fast" (non-fading after long exposure to strong light) or both.

Knitters often refer to the "hand" of the yarn, a term that applies to the softness and touch of the yarn. Better quality yarns feel more luxurious and much softer, because more softeners are added during the dyeing process.

"Bulk" describes the thickness and cover or furriness of yarn and, like the nap in a carpet, can range from short and tight (low bulk) to thick and plushy (high bulk). High bulk yarns make softer, warmer garments and blankets.

Another important factor to consider is the elasticity of the yarn, or the ability of yarn to stretch and spring back to its original shape. The reason for requiring good elasticity is simple: it prevents the garment from sagging or stretching. An easy way to check on elasticity is to stretch out a 12 inch length of yarn which should measure about 13¾ to 15½ inches. Let the yarn snap back; with good recovery it will again measure 12 inches, or close to it.

A similar factor is "resiliency," which is the ability of yarn to bounce out to its original shape and size after being crushed. The importance of resiliency is to prevent that limp, wrinkled, matted-down appearance when an article has been used or worn only a time or two. To check resiliency, crush a handful of yarn and see how it snaps back out when released.

Some projects specify 2-ply yarn, others 3-ply or 4-ply. The number of plies means the number of strands that are twisted together to form a length of yarn.

———————●———————

Here's a thumbnail description of the most popular types of yarn fibers:

ANIMAL FIBERS (all subject to shrinkage with improper laundering or drying)

ALPACA: Llama wool; fine textured, hard wearing.

ANGORA: Angora rabbit fur, plushy, warm and lightweight.

CASHMERE: Kashmir goat wool; extremely soft, warm and silky.

MOHAIR: Angora goat wool; long-fibered, durable and lustrous.

WOOL: Sheep's wool; warm, durable, absorbent, resilient.

VEGETABLE FIBERS (somewhat subject to shrinkage unless otherwise specified)

COTTON: From the cotton plant; soft, lightweight, cool and absorbent.

LINEN: From the flax plant; strong, lustrous, absorbent and durable.

MAN-MADE FIBERS (slight tendency to stretch or elongate in time)

ACRYLICS: Machine wash/dry, warm, resilient.

METALLICS: Decorative only, may discolor or be scratchy.

NYLON: Strong, lustrous, resilient.

POLYESTER: Machine wash/dry, strong, lustrous.

RAYON: Absorbent, lustrous, usually blended with other fibers.

———————————●———————————

Advanced technology in American yarn mills has allowed the intermixing of certain of these fibers to make all manner of combinations to accent warmth or coolness, ruggedness or daintiness, luxuriance or economy—an almost endless parade of variations to please nearly every popular whim.

There are four generally accepted weight categories for yarn: Light, Medium, Heavy and Extra Heavy. Brand labels may use other terms like "Bulky" or "Super Bulk" in describing various degrees of the Extra Heavy weight, for example. The following list gives examples of other names for the four weight classes, and items commonly knitted from each.

LIGHT WEIGHT (Baby yarn, fingering yarn, crochet cotton)

Infant wear, socks, doilies, scarves.

MEDIUM WEIGHT (Sport yarn)

Children's wear, light afghans, heavy socks, hats, sweaters, bedspreads.

HEAVY WEIGHT (Knitting worsted weight)

Afghans, outerwear, heavy sweaters, sportswear, blankets.

EXTRA HEAVY WEIGHT (Bulky)

Heavy afghans, rugs, extra heavy sweaters, jackets.

Yarn is packaged in skeins, balls or cones. Sometimes the length or yardage is given on the label, but because yarn is sold by its actual weight, you'll always find the weight of the package in ounces or metric measures; occasionally both. Here are common equivalents for our standard U.S. ounces and metric grams:

OUNCES to GRAMS	
¼ ounce =	7.78 grams
½ ounce =	15.55 grams
¾ ounce =	23.32 grams
1 ounce =	31.10 grams
1½ ounces =	46.65 grams
2 ounces =	62.21 grams
3 ounces =	93.31 grams
4 ounces =	124.41 grams

GRAMS to OUNCES	
1 gram =	.035 ounce
10 grams =	.35 ounce
20 grams =	.7 ounce
25 grams =	.88 ounce
30 grams =	1.05 ounces
40 grams =	1.4 ounces
50 grams =	1.75 ounces
100 grams =	3.5 ounces

A word of caution. Where the instructions call for a specific amount of a particular brand (perhaps not available in your area, thus forcing a substitution) always buy extra with the right to return unbroken packages, because there can be a wide variance in yardage for the same number of ounces (grams) when similar yarn is made by different manufacturers.

In any event it's always best to buy extra yarn so you're assured of enough of the right dye lot to finish your project.

Understanding Knitting Instructions, Terms, Abbreviations And Symbols

Knitting instructions often are confusing to beginners and appear to be written in some kind of mysterious code. Don't be intimidated, you'll soon understand knitting language right along with the experts.

The purpose of knitting language is to speed up the reading, following and understanding of printed instructions by condensing and shortening them through the use of a few key words or phrases, abbreviations and symbols. These are standard signals for the craft that enable you to follow knitting patterns, no matter the source.

It is important that you read through all of these terms before going to the next section. You can always refer back until you've committed everything to memory through repeated use. It's really quite simple and, if you're a crocheter, you'll recognize some common terms immediately, as many also are used in crocheting.

The terms are listed alphabetically.

BLOCK
Form pieces into proper shape by hand or with the aid of steam or pressing.

END RIGHT SIDE
Complete a row of the face or right side of the work before going on to the next step.

END WRONG SIDE
Complete a row of the back or wrong side of the work before going on to the next step.

GAUGE
The number of stitches to the inch horizontally and the number of rows to the inch vertically.

MARK ROW OR MARK STITCH
Loosely tie a contrasting piece of yarn or place a marker or safety pin at the beginning or at the end of a row or stitch.

MULTIPLE
Refers to the exact number of stitches needed to complete one pattern design. A multiple of 3 would be any number divisible by 3, such as 6, 9, 12. A multiple of 3 plus 1 would have one more stitch than a multiple of 3; for example 7, 10, 13.

RIGHT SIDE
The side that is seen in the finished article.

TURN
Turn the work around so the reverse side now faces you to begin the next step.

WORK EVEN
Continue working the pattern without increasing or decreasing the row length by adding or omitting any stitches.

WRONG SIDE
The reverse of the right side.

Standard Knitting Abbreviations:

CC	Contrasting Color
dec	decrease(s)(d)(ing)
inc	increase(s)(d)(ing)
k	knit
lp	loop
MC	Main Color
p	purl
psso	pass slip stitch over
rnd	round
sk	skip
sl	slip
sp	space
st	stitch
tog	together
yo	yarn over

In knitting instructions various symbols are used wherever a step is to be repeated. Because different originators of knitting patterns prefer to use different symbols for repeats, the symbols most often used are explained here.

———————●———————

ASTERISK* DOUBLE ASTERISK** and DAGGER†. These indicate the very same thing—beginning of a sequence that is to be repeated the number of times (in addition to the first) called for in the instructions. For example: *K 4, p 6, repeat from * twice, means to knit 4 stitches then purl 6 stitches—do this two more times (the original plus two repeats).

———————●———————

PARENTHESES () and BRACKETS []. Both indicate that the instructions contained within them are to be repeated. Brackets normally are used only when the repeat inside them is contained within a parenthetical step being repeated. For example: ([]).

———————●———————

It's an excellent idea to place markers of some sort on the work at the beginning and end of the sequence to be repeated. This will enable you to look back at the work completed. Additional markers will aid in keeping the proper count and in rechecking each step for accuracy before continuing.

At the beginning of any set of instructions to knit, you'll find gauge (the number of stitches to the inch and the number of rows to the inch). To stress the importance of using the right gauge, WORKBASKET Magazine editors include the phrase "TO SAVE TIME, TAKE TIME TO CHECK GAUGE" in their knitting instruction. Here's why.

The specified needle and yarn size should result in the given gauge. However, using the same needles and yarn, two different people may get a different gauge, due to a difference in the looseness or tightness of their stitches. You may need to adjust your needle size as follows.

The first step in following any instructions is to knit a sample swatch, about four inches square, following the pattern and using the yarn and the size needle specified. Now lay your sample on a hard flat surface and press it flat, being sure not to stretch it in any direction. Using a ruler (there is a knitting gauge printed on the back cover of this handbook), compare the gauge given in the instructions to the gauge of your sample swatch. Marking the 2 inch spans with pins may make counting easier and more accurate.

If your swatch has TOO FEW stitches or rows to the inch, then you work too loosely. Rip out your sample and make a new one using a SMALLER needle for the proper gauge.

If your swatch has TOO MANY stitches or rows to the inch, then you work too tightly. Rip out what you've done and make a new sample using a LARGER needle until you get the right gauge.

As you can see, yarn weight might be changed; needle size could be changed; but the thing that really matters is to be certain your work matches the gauge specified in the instructions. Remember too, that we often work more tightly when we are tense, so check your gauge from time to time reducing the need to rip out.

To summarize what we've covered in this chapter, printed instructions are a sort of "shorthand recipe" for knitting. To be sure the finished article will be the proper size, we should save ourselves a lot of time, trouble and frustration by checking the gauge often. Now let's go on to the mechanics of knitting.

Learning To Knit The Simple Way

There is no substitute for *doing* when it comes to learning to knit, so the quicker you get started, the easier it will be to learn. If you have someone around who already knows how to knit and who can give you pointers—so much the better.

Knitting, like tying one's shoes or playing the piano, is a two-handed activity for left-handed or right-handed individuals. One doesn't write from right to left because of being left-handed, nor is there such a thing as left-handed music or left-handed knitting patterns. True, you may find it awkward at first to knit as right-handers do, but so do right-handed people, and this way *everyone* can help you because they'll see things the same way you do. Even if you decide you prefer to carry the yarn in your left hand as in the "European method" of knitting, you can still make your stitches and bring your yarn over in the same direction as right-handers do. The important thing is the end result— that you learn to knit in a way that's best, most comfortable and enjoyable for *you.*

To eliminate confusion as we get into the actual details of knitting we shall refer to the right hand and the left hand in all instructions and this will apply no matter which hand is favored.

Reduced to its simplest form, knitting is nothing more than making a series of yarn loops and interlacing them in various ways to form patterns. It's entirely possible to do this with some yarn by just using your fingers— as in tying knots. Therefore, concentrate on the yarn and what is happening to it, or what you want it to do; don't become self-conscious about hand positions, finger movements or needle positions. These should become easy and routine if you are concentrating more on what you are creating than on what you are using to do it. Knitting needles are extensions of your fingers; thus needles and hands become your knitting machine.

For practice, take some knitting worsted weight yarn in a bright, pleasing color. Use a pair of number 8 aluminum or plastic knitting needles in a sharply contrasting color so you can study what's happening to the yarn as you work.

Before we begin, it's important to note that we'll be using knitting terms, abbreviations and symbols increasingly, so you can become more and more familiar with them as you see them used in actual practice.

The first step in any knitting project is to get some basic stitches looped onto a knitting needle to serve as a foundation for the stitches that will be added on top. Putting these basic stitches on the needle is known as casting on.

CASTING ON

Casting on can be done in several ways. The two explained here are

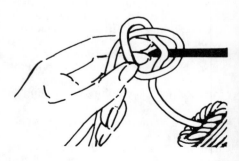

Make a slipknot 15″ from end of yarn and place on needle, pulling both ends to tighten—this counts as one stitch.

considered the most popular. In using the one-needle method, one must determine in advance how many stitches to cast on. That raises the next question; how much yarn to allow. This also is easy to determine. Loosely wind the same number of turns around your needle as you'll need cast on stitches, plus above five more turns. Make a slipknot at the last turn you put on, slide the coiled yarn off the needle (the slip knot stays on) and you've not only measured yarn, but also cast on the first stitch.

CASTING ON, ONE-NEEDLE METHOD

To practice, measure off enough yarn for 20 cast on stitches (we'll call this the tail end) and place a slip knot on the needle. Now grasp the needle loosely in the right hand with the tail end of the yarn toward you and the ball end away from you. Loop loose end of yarn over left thumb and other end of yarn over index finger, bring both ends of yarn down across palm and hold yarns with remaining fingers (Step 1). Bring needle under yarn on left thumb (Step 2), across and pick up yarn on index finger (Step 3), draw yarn through under thumb dropping thumb yarn, tighten (loop stitch) on needle and place thumb in same position as at beginning (Step 4). Repeat for desired number of stitches.

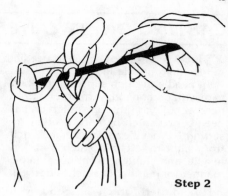

Step 2

Insert needle into loop on thumb from front to back.

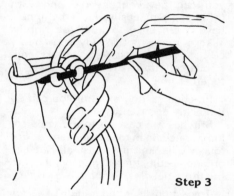

Step 3

Wind yarn in right hand over point of needle from back to front.

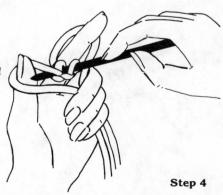

Step 4

Pass point of needle through loop on thumb from back to front, easing loop off thumb.

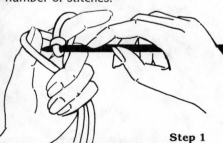

Step 1

Hold needle in right hand with yarn from skein running over index finger. With left hand hold end of yarn in palm with last three fingers. Loop yarn around left thumb.

CASTING ON, TWO-NEEDLE METHOD

Place a slipknot on left needle. Holding needle in left hand, insert right needle through slip knot, pick up yarn with other hand, yarn around right needle, pull yarn through stitch on left needle (one stitch on each needle). Inserting left needle through right stitch from right to left, slip stitch onto left needle and tighten. Continue in this manner for number of stitches desired.

No matter which method you choose, be sure all your stitches (sts) are facing the right way and above all that they are made loosely enough so you can get your needle and yarn through them easily. Most beginners have a tendency to knot too tightly. Take a moment to study your newly cast on stitches (sts) so you are conscious of how the yarn loops fit together.

Practice casting on until you can do it quickly and easily.

Stitches are cast on to a circular or jumper needle in the same manner. For four-needle knitting, cast all stitches on one needle; then divide evenly onto the three needles, forming a triangle.

To cast on sts in the middle of a project, with the right side of the work facing you cast on by using the two-needle method.

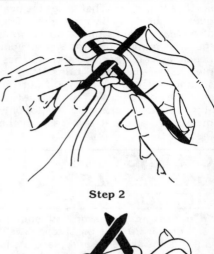

Step 2

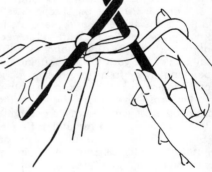

Step 3

Step 1

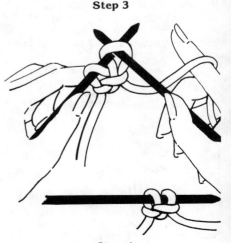

Step 4

KNIT STITCH (k)
AMERICAN STYLE

As in casting on, you again have optional methods of knitting to consider. To learn the American style, cast on 20 stitches. Holding needle with cast on stitches in left hand, insert right needle into bottom of the first stitch on the left needle, going from the front to back of left needle. Slide the right needle through and upward until the broadest part of the needle rises well above and behind the left needle to form a needle cross. Holding both needles with left fingers, pick up yarn in right hand. Drape around back of index finger, letting yarn fall across or around the other fingers to the ball. Position of yarn will be a matter of personal preference. Find what works for you. This draping around your fingers helps to regulate the yarn tension. Now, with the yarn in the back, wrap it counterclockwise around the right needle. (The yarn is now between the two needles.) Hold the yarn snugly and carefully draw yarn through stitch on left needle, making a loop on right needle. The point of the right needle comes down and back up in front of the left needle. Slip worked stitch off left needle. Right needle now holds your first knit (k) stitch (st). The yarn will be in back, ready to start the second st. Repeat the process in each st on the left needle until it is empty. Then the right hand needle, holding all the sts, will be switched to the left hand and the process repeated. By repeating the knit stitch for several rows, you will have formed what is called the GARTER STITCH. Take a moment to study what you have done. Are your stitches even, uniformly sized, smooth, all facing the same direction? A common error is to work on the points of the needles rather than being sure that the fat part of the needle is used to "size" each st properly as it is formed.

Insert point of empty needle through front of first cast on stitch from front to back, passing right needle under left needle. Always keep yarn BEHIND work when making knit stitch.

Wrap yarn from skein counterclockwise around point of right needle.

Draw wrapped yarn through first stitch by bringing right needle down, under and up in front of left needle. Right needle holds new loop.

Slide old stitch off left needle—one stitch made.

KNIT STITCH (k)
EUROPEAN STYLE

In this style of knitting, the only difference is that the yarn is held and worked from the left hand instead of the right. Holding a needle with 20 cast on stitches in your right hand, and with the palm of your left hand facing you, drape the ball end yarn from the last cast on st on the needle over the top of your left index finger, across the palm side of your next three fingers and take a turn around your little finger. Keeping the yarn behind the work, take an empty needle in your right hand and insert it from right to left into the lp on the left-hand needle of the first cast on st in line. Slide the needle right through and upward until the broadest part of it rises well above and behind the left needle to form a needle cross. In a counterclockwise motion with the left index finger, wrap the ball end yarn around the right-hand needle one full turn (yo) and hold it snugly. It is now between the two needles. Complete the st and continue exactly as detailed under the American method.

Note: Regardless of which method you prefer, there should be absolutely no difference in the final results. The main thing is to choose whichever style is easiest and most comfortable for you, and practice until you feel confident.

Never leave your work until you finish a row. Cap the needle point with a point protector to safeguard completed sts.

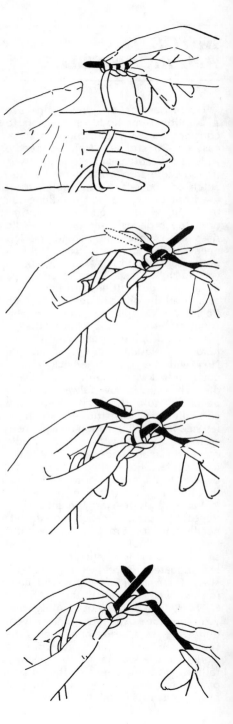

PURL STITCH (p)

The **purl (p) stitch** is the only other stitch you need to learn. All other sts are merely combinations of knitting and purling, which is a pleasant surprise to most beginners. Therefore, learn to purl well; it's really quite easy to learn if you realize that purling is like knitting *backwards.*

To start, cast on 20 sts and hold your needles as if you were going to knit (or you can purl onto your last knitted row). Keep the yarn *in front of* your work at all times when purling, instead of in back as when knitting. Insert the empty right-hand needle into the lp of the first st from *right to left* and position

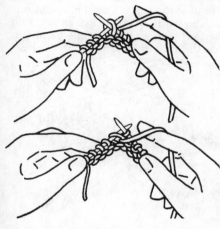

the right-hand needle *in front of* the left hand needle (again the opposite of knitting). With a counterclockwise motion, wrap the yarn between the two needles and continue around the right needle (yo); complete the stitch as in knitting.

Purling is rarely used alone, but is used constantly in combination with knitting. When you've completed a practice row of purling, knit the next row, then purl the next. Alternating rows of knitting with rows of purling is known as the STOCKINETTE STITCH. Continue until you have purling down pat.

TO SLIP A STITCH (sl)

Insert the **right-hand needle** into the next stitch as if to purl (unless instructed otherwise), *do not yarn over,* merely slip the stitch off the left needle and onto the right needle without either knitting or purling it.

INCREASING (inc)

To **increase** in *knitting* or *purling,* work one stitch, but do not slip the stitch off the left needle; instead, work into the back loop of the same stitch (thereby making two stitches out of one), then slip the stitch off the needle.

DECREASING (dec)

To **decrease** in *knitting* or *purling,* insert the right needle into the loops of the next *two* stitches, yarn over (thereby making one stitch out of two), slip the stitch off the needle and proceed. *Or,* slip one stitch, knit or purl one stitch, then pass the slipped stitch over (psso) the knitted or purled stitch.

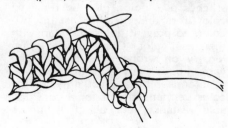

BINDING OFF

To prevent a finished piece from unraveling, instructions will call for binding off a number of stitches. To bind off, knit two stitches onto the right hand needle in the usual manner.

*Insert the left hand needle from left to right into the top loop of the first stitch you just knitted across, lift it over the top of the second stitch and let it drop off between the needles (one stitch remains on the right needle). Knit another stitch (again two stitches on right needle). Repeat from * until desired stitches are bound off. Then clip the yarn about four inches beyond the last stitch, feed the end through the last stitch on the right hand needle and pull firmly. When binding off, keep stitches loose to prevent distortion. Always bind off in pattern stitch being worked unless otherwise instructed.

JOINING YARN

When you need to start a new skein of yarn, or cut out a bad place in the yarn, here are three proven methods of joining. The best way is to drop the end of yarn at the beginning of a row, leaving about a two inch length and begin working with the new yarn, leaving a two inch length. After the article is finished, thread the yarn end in a blunt needle and weave it in and out for 8 or 10 stitches.

You also can join yarn at the end of a row by making a slipknot with the new strand around the previous strand. Draw slipknot close to end of work.

Another way is to work within 4 inches of end of yarn, then lay a new strand along the old so that about one inch extends beyond last stitch. Knit the four stitches with double yarn, cutting the ends after completion of piece.

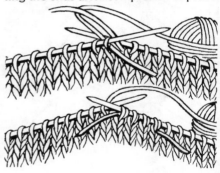

CHANGING COLORS

When you are working with two or more colors, the yarns should be twisted at the back of the work when changing from one color to the next. After knitting the required number of stitches of a color, pick up the next color from underneath, twist the two colors to prevent holes and start with the new color. Carry unused yarn loosely on wrong side, twisting the yarn in back every few stitches to prevent loops in back. If you are ending a color permanently, or for a considerable distance, cut about 4 inches

beyond the last stitch in which it is used and follow the procedure for joining new yarn. This is the procedure used in Fair Isle knitting.

RIBBING

An alternating number of knit and purl stitches (for example: knit 2, purl 2) results in ribbing which, because of its elastic quality, is used for lower edges of sweaters, cuffs, necklines and tops of gloves or socks. In knit 2, purl 2 ribbing, the number of stitches cast on is usually divisible by four. Knit the first 2 stitches, bring the yarn forward and purl 2 stitches, then bring the yarn back of needle and knit 2 stitches. Continue in this manner to end of row.

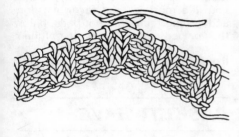

PICKING UP STITCHES

A crochet hook is usually used to pick up stitches around the neck and armholes of apparel projects. Hold work with right side toward you and work from right to left. Insert a crochet hook into the first row in from the edge and draw yarn through, thus forming a stitch, which then is placed on the knitting needle. Repeat around until the desired number of stitches have been picked up. When picking up stitches on an irregular edge be sure to pick up a stitch in every row. Divide a large, rounded area into four sections (using

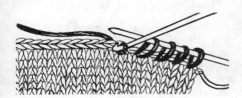

contrasting yarn or pins). This way you will be certain to pick up one-fourth of the stitches in each section, thus giving a smooth-finished surface. To prevent holes, go through 2 strands of the stitch.

FILLING IN DROPPED STITCHES

In stockinette or rib stitch pick up a stitch on right side of work. Insert a crochet hook in the dropped stitch, draw yarn to row above through loop forming a loop. Continue in this manner until you reach the row being worked. Be careful and do not twist the stitches. Pick up purl sts as shown in illustration.

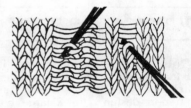

MAKING BUTTONHOLES

Work to the place specified for a buttonhole, then bind off number of sts specified in directions and work to the end of the row. In the next row work to the bound off stitches and cast on the same number of stitches bound off in the previous row; complete the row.

SEAMING BY WEAVING

With the right side up, hold the edges of the pieces to be joined together. Thread a tapestry needle and insert it in the center of the stitch on the right edge, pass under two rows,

20

draw yarn through to the right side. Insert the needle in the corresponding row of the left edge, draw yarn through in the same way. Continue to work in this manner from side to side, matching rows or patterns. Be careful not to pull the yarn too tight. A long-lasting seam should have elasticity.

DUPLICATE STITCH

This is a type of embroidery stitch that is worked over the stockinette stitch and gives the same effect as a knitted-in design. Use a large blunt needle with a fairly large eye. Thread with contrasting yarn and from the wrong side bring the needle to the right side through the center of the stitch. Follow the outline of the knit stitch, draw the yarn across the back of the two strands of this stitch, bring the needle back to the center of the same stitch and draw the yarn through. When forming the next stitch, bring the needle through the center of the stitch just completed—see sketch.

Fig. 1   Fig. 2

Useful Pattern Stitches

These are a few of the more popular of the hundreds of pattern stitches. Beginners especially are urged to make up sample swatches of various patterns for practice. You may enjoy making up squares of pattern stitches you like most in your favorite colors and joining them into hot pads, pillow tops or perhaps your very first afghan.

The various pattern stitches are listed here alphabetically for your convenience.

BASKETWEAVE

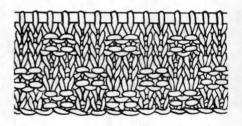

Cast on any number of stitches divisible by 4.

Rows 1, 2: *K 2, p 2, repeat from * across.
Row 3: K.
Rows 4, 5: *P 2, k 2, repeat from * across.
Row 6: P.
These 6 rows form the pattern.

By increasing the number of knitted and purled stitches (to 3 for example) and increasing the number of rows of like sequence (to 3 for example) you can simulate larger splints in the weave.

BLOCK STITCH

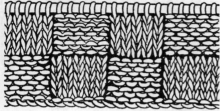

Cast on any number of stitches divisible by 10.

Row 1: K 5, p 5 across. Repeat this row 4 more times.

Row 6: P 5, k 5 across. Repeat this row 4 more times. Repeat these 10 rows for complete pattern.

CABLE STITCH

Cast on any number of stitches divisible by 10, plus 2.

Row 1: P 3, *k 6, p 4, repeat from * across, ending k 6, p 3.

Row 2: K 3, p 6, *k 4, p 6, repeat from * across, ending k 3. Repeat Rows 1 and 2 twice (6 rows in all).

Row 7: P 3, *slip next 3 sts onto a double pointed needle or cable hook and place in back of work, k next 3 sts, then k the 3 sts from double pointed needle (forms cable), p 4. Repeat from * across, ending with a cable and p 3.

Row 8: Repeat Row 2. Repeat these 8 rows for pattern.

DIAMOND WEAVE

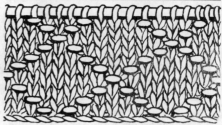

Cast on any number of stitches divisible by 8, plus one.

Row 1: K 4, *p 1, k 7, repeat from * across, ending p 1, k 4.

Row 2: P 3, *k 1, p 1, k 1, p 5, repeat from * across, ending p 3.

Row 3: K 2, *p 1, k 3, repeat from * across, ending k 2.

Row 4: P 1, *k 1, p 5, k 1, p 1, repeat from * across, ending p 1.

Row 5: *P 1, k 7, repeat from * across, ending p 1.

Row 6: P 1, *k 1, p 5, k 1, p 1, repeat from * across, ending p 1.

Row 7: K 2, *p 1, k 3, repeat from * across, ending k 2.

Row 8: P 3, *k 1, p 1, k 1, p 5, repeat from * across, ending p 3. Repeat these 8 rows for pattern.

EYELET MESH

Cast on an odd number of stitches.

Row 1: P this row and all odd rows.

Row 2: K 1, *yo, k 2 tog, repeat from * across.

Row 4: K. Repeat from Row 1 for pattern.

HONEYCOMB STITCH

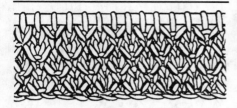

Cast on an even number of stitches.
Row 1: (Wrong Side) K.
Row 2: *K 1, k the next st and the same st below tog (pick up front lp of st below and next st on needle at same time), repeat from * across.
Row 3: K.
Row 4: *K the first st and the same st below tog, k 1, repeat from * across.
Repeat these 4 rows for pattern.

KNOT STITCH

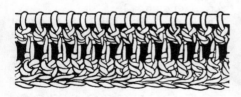

Cast on any number of stitches.
Row 1: *Yo twice, k 1, repeat from * across.
Row 2: *K 1, make 2 sts of the yarn overs (k one and p the other), then pass the first and second sts on the right hand needle over the third, repeat from * across. Repeat these 2 rows for pattern.

LACE STITCH WITH POINTED EDGE

Cast on any number of stitches divisible by 9.

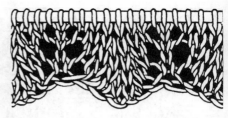

Row 1: *K 2 tog, k 2, yo, k 1, yo, k 2, k 2 tog, repeat from * across.
Row 2: P. These 2 rows form the pattern.

LEAF STITCH

Cast on any number of stitches divisible by 10, plus 3.
Row 1: K 5, *yo, sl 1, k 2 tog, psso, yo, k 7, repeat from * across, ending k 5.
Row 2: P this row and all even rows.
Row 3: K 2 tog, k 3, *yo, k 3, yo, k 2, sl 1, k 2 tog, psso, k 2, repeat from * across, ending with yo, k 3, yo, k 3, k 2 tog.
Row 5: K 2 tog, k 2, *yo, k 5, yo, k 1, sl 1, k 2 tog, psso, k 1, repeat from * across, ending with yo, k 5, yo, k 2, k 2 tog.

Row 7: K 2 tog, k 1, *yo, k 7, yo, sl 1, k 2 tog, psso, repeat from * across, ending with yo, k 7, yo, k 1, k 2 tog.

Row 9: K 3, *yo, k 2, sl 1, k 2 tog, psso, k 2, yo, k 3, repeat from * across.

Row 11: K 4, *yo, k 1, sl 1, k 2 tog, psso, k 1, yo, k 5, repeat from * across, ending with k 4.

Row 12: P. Repeat from Row 1 for pattern.

MOSS STITCH

(Also called seed stitch and sometimes rice stitch)

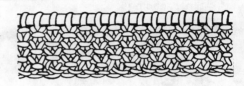

Cast on any uneven number of stitches.

Row 1: K 1, p 1 across. Repeat this row for pattern.

Aunt Ellen's Favorite Knitting Projects

For nearly half a century, Aunt Ellen has brought hundreds of practical and attractive knitting projects to The WORKBASKET Magazine readers. Selecting the *best* for inclusion here would be virtually impossible, so here are a few of her more popular favorites from over the years.

Each of these projects has been graded for degree of difficulty, and is rated either *Easy, Intermediate* or *Challenging,* as a guide.

PATCHWORK AFGHAN

Intermediate-Challenging

Five different pattern stitches are combined to make this attractive afghan. Use 4-ply knitting worsted and one pair number 8 knitting needles or any size needles that will result in stitch gauge given and a plastic crochet hook size H. You will need 4 ounces black, 22 ounces white, 4 ounces each of blue, rose-beige and gold, 5 ounces each gray and scarlet. The afghan is made in five strips combining the various pattern stitches. Each pattern stitch is numbered and

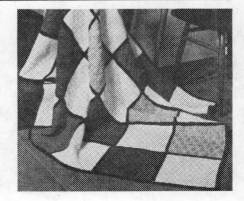

the chart shows suggested arrangement of color and pattern blocks. All like patterns are worked with the same color, on 36 stitches for 64 rows.

Gauge: 4 sts equal 1 inch

Matchstick Pattern—(Number 1)

Rows 1, 3, 5, 7: K.

Rows 2, 4, 6, 8: *K 5, p 1, repeat from * 4 times, ending k 6.

Seed Pattern—(Number 3)

Matchstick Pattern—(Number 1)

Rows 9, 11, 13, 15: K.

Rows 10, 12, 14, 16: K 2, p 1, *k 5, p 1, repeat from * 4 times, ending k 3. Repeat these 16 rows 3 times.

Checkerboard Pattern—(Number 2)

Rows 1, 3: K 4, *p 4, k 4, repeat from * 3 times.

Rows 2, 4: P 4, *k 4, p 4, repeat from * 3 times.

Cable Pattern—(Number 4)

Rows 2, 4, 6: P 5, k 2, *p 6, k 2, repeat from * twice, ending p 5.

Row 5: K 5, p 2, *sl next 3 sts on double pointed needle and hold in back of work, k next 3 sts, k 3 sts from double pointed needle, p 2, repeat from * twice, k 5. Repeat these 6 rows 9 times, then repeat first 4 rows.

Diamond Pattern—(Number 5)

Rows 1, 3: K 1, *p 4, k 8, repeat from * once, p 4, k 7.

Row 2: P 6, k 6, repeat from beginning twice.

Rows 4, 10: P 8, k 2, p 10, repeat from * once, k 2, p 2.

Rows 5, 9: K 8, p 2, *k 10, p 2, repeat from * once, k 2.

Rows 6, 8: P 1, k 4, *p 8, k 4, repeat from * once, p 7.

Checkerboard Pattern—(Number 2)

Rows 5, 7: P 4, *k 4, p 4, repeat from * 3 times.

Rows 6, 8: K 4, *p 4, k 4, repeat from * 3 times. Repeat these 8 rows 7 times.

Seed Pattern—(Number 3)

Row 1: K 1, p 1.

Row 2: P 1, k 1. Repeat these 2 rows 31 times.

Cable Pattern—(Number 4)

Rows 1, 3: K 5, p 2, *k 6, p 2, repeat from * twice, ending k 5.

Diamond Pattern—(Number 5)

Row 7: K 6, p 6, repeat from beginning twice. Repeat these 10 rows 5 times ending with first 4 rows.

The white pattern is worked in garter st (k 64 rows). Follow chart for all other color blocks (64 rows each).

First Strip: In black, cast on 36 sts. Work 4 rows in garter st (k each row), cut black. Join color of next pattern according to chart and work in pattern for 64 rows, cut color. Join black, k 4 rows, cut color. Join color of next pattern, complete pattern, cut color. Continue in this manner until all patterns for this strip have been completed, fasten off. Join black, k 3 rows, but do not cut yarn. Work a row of sc down long side working an sc in every other row, fasten off. Join black on other long side of strip and work a row of sc to correspond.

Work the other 4 strips to correspond, following chart for patterns—separate patterns with 4 k rows in black.

Finishing: Block each strip. Sew strips together with black working through back lps of sts only.

cable design afghan

Intermediate

This toasty-warm afghan, planned in the size and colors most appropriate for a little one's room, requires about 12 ounces white and 4 ounces each of six pastel colors in 4-ply knitting worsted weight yarn. Use standard knitting needles number 8 and cable stitch holder. Afghan measures about 31 x 42 inches. A larger size could be made if desired.

Afghan Strip: Cast on 18 sts. Work in pattern as follows:

Pattern: Rows 1, 3, 5, 7: (Wrong Side) K 2, p 2, k 2, p 6, k 2, p 2, k 2.
Rows 2, 4, 8: K 4, p 2, k 6, p 2, k 4.
Row 6: (Cable Twist) K 4, p 2, sl 3 sts to holder and hold in back of work, k 3, k 3 from holder, p 2, k 4.
Repeat 8 pattern rows until 35 cable twists have been made, end with 5 more pattern rows after last twist. Bind off.
Make 4 white and 6 pastel strips.

Finishing: Sew strips together with white strips between pastel strips.

Fringe: Wrap yarn around a 10 inch cardboard. Cut at both ends. Matching colors, knot a fringe in every third stitch across each end of afghan; trim fringe.

Block without stretching.

FIRST STRIP	SECOND STRIP	THIRD STRIP	FOURTH STRIP	FIFTH STRIP
White	#3 Gray	White	#5 Gold	White
#4 Blue	White	#1 Rose Beige	White	#3 Gray
White	#2 Scarlet	White	#4 Blue	White
#3 Gray	White	#5 Gold	White	#2 Scarlet
White	#1 Rose Beige	White	#3 Gray	White
#2 Scarlet	White	#4 Blue	White	1# Rose Beige
White	#5 Gold	White	#2 Scarlet	White

WHITE SQUARES ARE KNIT IN GARTER STITCH

BABY BOOTIES

Easy

To fit a newborn baby, use number 8 needles; for 6 month's size, use number 9 needles. Booties take about one ounce knitting worsted and, if desired, a small amount of contrasting color for tie cord. Use size H crochet hook.

Gauge: On number 8 needles:
    4 sts equal 1 inch
    10 rows garter st equal 1 inch
    On number 9 needles:
    7 sts equal 2 inches
    8 rows garter st equal 1 inch

With MC, cast on 34 sts.

Next 12 Rows: Work in garter st (k each row—makes 6 ridges).

Instep Shaping: Row 1: K 15, (k 2 tog) twice (2 sts dec), k 15—32 sts.

Row 2 and All Even Rows: K.

Row 3: K 14, (k 2 tog) twice, k 14—30 sts.

Rows 5, 7, 9, 11: Continue to k across to center 4 sts, (k 2 tog) twice, k to end —22 sts at end of Row 11.

Row 13: (Eyelet Row) Insert needle in first st as for a k st, wrap yarn around needle twice, then complete the st, continue in same way in each st across.

Row 14: P across, pulling off and not working the extra lp of each st (makes long sts).

Next 8 Rows: *K 1, p 1 in ribbing, repeat from * across.

Bind off in ribbing. Sew back and foot seam.

Make second bootie to match.

Cord: (Make 2) With CC and crochet hook, make a chain approximately 18 inches long. Fasten off. Lace cord through long sts (eyelets) at ankle. Tie at center front. Knot ends of tie.

NURSING BOTTLE COVER

Easy

For bottle cover, you need about 70 yards medium pink and 10 yards buttercup in heavy rug yarn, one pair standard knitting needles number 10½, large-eye needle, plastic crochet hook size J, one 7 inch pink skirt zipper, ¾ yard narrow ribbon, ½ yard medium blue ribbon, scraps of black and red felt, filling material and a baby bottle.

Gauge: 3 sts equal 1 inch

BODY AND HEAD: With pink, cast on 22 sts. K each row until work measures 10 inches, bind off.

Thread yarn into blunt needle and gather cast on edge together tightly for bottom.

Sew zipper in side seam, sewing remainder of seam together. Gather

tightly, directly above zipper, for neck. Fill head; gather top together tightly.

ARMS: (Make 2) With pink, cast on 10 sts. K each row until work measures 3 inches, bind off. Sew seam; gather one end tightly together. Fill and attach to body.

Hair: With buttercup, ch 4, join to form a ring, sl st in ring, *sc in ring, draw yarn through lp and up to a 2½ inch length, hold lp on hook, repeat from * 19 times, dropping lps when necessary, fasten off. Work a second lp group with 12 lps only, fasten off. Attach 12-lp group on top of 20-lp group and attach to top of head.

Face: Cut features from felt as shown in photograph; sew in place. Insert bottle.

INFANT'S SLEEPER BAG

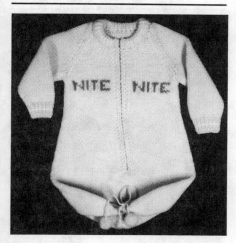

Challenging

Changing baby is a breeze with this drawstring bottom sleeper bag. It requires about 8 ounces pastel and small amounts of white and blue 4-ply knitting worsted weight yarn, standard knitting needles numbers 5 and 8 or any size needles which work to gauge. Use bobbins and 12 inch zipper.

Gauge: 5 sts equal 1 inch
7 rows equal 1 inch

BACK: With larger needles, cast on 13 sts for lower edge.

Rows 1, 3, 5, 7: P.

Row 2: K across, inc one st in every second st, end k 1—19 sts.

Row 4: K across, inc one st in every second st, end k 1—28 sts.

Row 6: K across, inc one st in every second st, end with an inc in last st—42 sts.

Row 8: K across, inc one st in every second st, end with an inc in last st—63 sts.

Work in stockinette (k 1 row, p 1 row) until back is 7 inches.

Dec one st each end of needle every 6th row 6 times—51 sts.

Continue to work in stockinette until 4 inches above last dec, ending with p row.

Armhole and Raglan Shaping: Bind off 2 sts at beginning of next 2 rows.

K 1, k 2 tog, k to 3 sts from end, sl 1, k 1, psso, k 1. Repeat last row every k row until 19 sts remain.

Sl sts to holder for back of neck.

FRONT: Work exactly the same as back to first dec row. Work first dec row as follows: K 2 tog, k 29, k 2 tog, k 28, k 2 tog—60 sts.

Row 1: P 27, k 1, p 1, k 1—last 3 sts are seed st border. Join another skein of yarn and k 1, p 1, k 1 (seed st border for other front), p to end.

Row 2: K to last 3 sts, k 1, p 1, k 1 (border sts), pick up other skein of yarn and k 1, p 1, k 1 (border sts), k to end of row.

Repeat last 2 rows, working dec one st each end of needle every 6th row 6

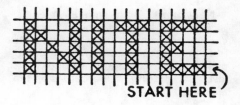

START HERE

times, until 3 inches above last dec row, ending with p row.

K 4 sts, join blue and work first row of letters from chart, other front work 3 border sts, k 2 and join blue and work letters from chart.

Note: When changing color, always hold color which has just been worked to the left and pick up new color from underneath. This twists the colors and eliminates a hole.

Complete chart and work armhole and raglan shaping as on back, until 6 raglan dec have been worked.

Neck Shaping: K to last 5 sts of left front and sl these sts onto a holder, work across the first 5 sts of right front and sl these sts onto a holder.

Dec one st at each neck edge every k row 4 times, continuing raglan dec until no sts remain.

SLEEVES: With smaller needles, cast on 30 sts.

K 1, p 1 in ribbing for ½ inch, ending on wrong side, fasten off pink. Join white and work 2 rows (when changing color on ribbing always k or p first row of new color, then continue in ribbing), fasten off white. Join pink and work ½ inch.

Change to larger needles and work in stockinette, inc one st each end of needle every inch 5 times—40 sts. Work even until sleeve length is 7 or desired inches.

Raglan Shaping: Bind off 2 sts at beginning of next 2 rows. Dec one st each end of needle every k row 14 times. Sl remaining 8 sts to a holder.

Finishing: Sew sleeves to front and back pieces and sew side seams and sleeve seams.

Neckband: With smaller needles, pick up and k 65 sts around neck including sts from holders. (Sl first 5 sts from holder to needle and then start picking up sts along neck edge, work last 5 sts working the border sts on the last 3 sts).

Next Row: Work border sts, p 1, *k 1, p 1, repeat from * to last 3 sts, work border.

Continue to work border sts and ribbing for ½ inch. Work border sts in pink and join white and work 2 rows of ribbing, fasten off white and join pink and work 1¼ inches. Bind off sts loosely in ribbing. Fold neck ribbing double and loosely sew in place to wrong side.

Finishing: Work in ends and block. Sew zipper by hand under the seed st borders.

Make cord and run through each cast on st at bottom of sacque. Make pompoms and sew to each end of cord. Draw cord up tight and tie in bow.

Cord: Cut a strand of yarn 40 inches long. Fasten one end securely to a stationary object. Twist strand tightly. Bring the 2 ends together, allowing yarn to twist upon itself and tie loose end in a knot, then tie a knot in the other end. Sew pompom to each end.

THUMBLESS BABY MITTENS

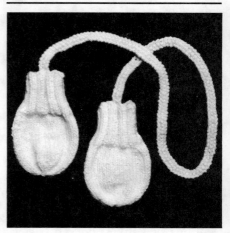

Intermediate

These baby mittens joined with a tie will never get lost. Mittens require about ½ ounce 2-ply acrylic sport weight yarn and one set number 2 double pointed needles.

Mittens: (Make 2) Cast on 36 sts and divide evenly on three needles.

Rnds 1 through 15: Work in k 2, p 2 ribbing around, place marker at end of rnd.

Rnds 16, 17: K.

Rnd 18: Inc one st in first st, k 17, inc one st in next st, k 17—38 sts.

Rnds 19, 20: Work even in k.

Rnd 21: Inc one st in first st, k 18, inc one st in next st, k 18—40 sts.

Work even next 15 rnds.

Dec Rnd: *K 1, k 2 tog, repeat from * around, ending k 1—27 sts.

Work even in k on next 2 rnds.

Second Dec Rnd: K 2 tog repeated around ending with k 1—14 sts.

Next Rnd: Work even in k.

Finishing: Cut thread and pull through remaining sts. Pull together, fasten off.

Tie: Cast on 3 sts.

Pattern Row: P 1, k 1, p 1.

Repeat pattern row until tie measures 18 or desired inches. Fasten tie to cuffs of mittens.

INFANT SNOWSUIT

Challenging

This snowsuit with an owl design will look adorable on your infant. A zipper, with opening end placed at waist, extends from waist up through hood on back of sweater. Directions are for size 1 with any changes for sizes 2 and 3 in parentheses. You need about 10 ounces of medium weight sport yarn, one pair each standard knitting needles numbers 3 and 5 and one set double pointed needles number 3 or size needed for gauge, 18 (18, 20) inch zipper, twelve 5/16 inch buttons, 1/2 inch wide elastic, elastic thread and black yarn or thread.

Gauge: 6 sts equal 1 inch
8 rows equal 1 inch

Pattern for Panel and Owl Design for Front of Sweater: Row 1: K 10 (12, 14)—first panel, p 1, *k 8, p 1—panel, repeat from * 3 times, k 10 (12, 14).

Row 2: P 10 (12, 14), k 1, *p 8, k 1, repeat from * 3 times, p 10 (12, 14).

Row 3: (Begin First Owl) K 10 (12, 14), p 10—owl sts, (k 8, p 1) 3 times, k 10 (12, 14).

Rows 4, 5, 6: Repeat Rows 2, 1 and 2.

Row 7: (Owl Cable Patterns) K 10 (12, 14), p 1, sl 2 sts to double pointed needle and hold in BACK of work, k 2 sts, k 2 sts from double pointed needle, sl 2 sts to double pointed needle and hold in FRONT of work, k 2 sts, k 2 sts from double pointed needle, p 1, (k 8, p 1) 3 times, k 10 (12, 14).

Rows 8 through 16: Work Rows 2 and 1 in established panel design.

Row 17: Repeat Row 7.

Rows 18, 20, 22: Repeat Row 2.

Rows 19, 21: Repeat Row 1.

Row 23: Repeat Row 7.

Rows 24, 26: Repeat Row 2.

Row 25: Repeat Row 1.

Row 27: (Second and Third Owls) K 10 (12, 14), p 1, k 8, p 19—owl sts, k 8, p 1, k 10 (12, 14).

Rows 28, 30: Repeat Row 2.

Row 29: Repeat Row 1.

Row 31: K 10 (12, 14), p 1, k 8, *p 1, sl 2 sts to double pointed needle and hold in BACK of work, k 2 sts, k 2 sts from double pointed needle, sl 2 sts to double pointed needle and hold in FRONT of work, k 2 sts, k 2 sts from double pointed needle, repeat from * once, p 1, k 8, p 1, k 10 (12, 14).

Rows 32, 34, 36, 38, 40: Repeat Row 2.

Rows 33, 35, 37, 39: Repeat Row 1.

Row 41: Repeat Row 31.

Rows 42, 44, 46: Repeat Row 2.

Rows 43, 45: Repeat Row 1.

Row 47: Repeat Row 31.

Rows 48, 50: Repeat Row 2.

Row 49: Repeat Row 1.

Row 51: (Fourth Owl) K 10 (12, 14), *p 1, k 8, repeat from * twice, p 10—owl sts, k 10 (12, 14).

Rows 52, 54: Repeat Row 2.

Row 53: Repeat Row 1.

Row 55: K 10 (12, 14), p 1, *k 8, p 1, repeat from * twice, sl 2 sts to double pointed needle and hold in BACK of work, k 2 sts, k 2 sts from double pointed needle, sl 2 sts to double pointed needle and hold in FRONT of work, k 2 sts, k 2 sts from double pointed needle, p 1, k 10 (12, 14).

Rows 56, 58, 60, 62, 64: Repeat Row 2.

Rows 57, 59, 61, 63: Repeat Row 1.

Row 65: Repeat Row 55.

Rows 66, 68, 70: Repeat Row 2.

Rows 67, 69: Repeat Row 1.

Row 71: Repeat Row 55.

Row 72: Repeat Row 2.

Continue Rows 1 and 2 through binding off sts at shoulder.

SWEATER FRONT: Using smaller needles, cast on 57 (61, 65) sts. Work in k 1, p 1 ribbing for 9 rows. Change to larger needles, work panel pattern rows and place owls. When work measures 7½ (8, 8½) inches from beginning, shape armholes.

To Shape Armholes: At beginning of each of next 2 rows bind off 2 st. Dec one st each end of needle every other row 1 (2, 2) times. On Rows 65 and 71 work owl patterns. Work on 51 (53, 57) sts until armhole measures 3 (3¼, 3½) inches or desired length.

Shape Neck: Work 17 (18, 20) sts, sl next 17 sts to holder, join another ball of yarn and work 17 (18, 20) sts. Dec one st each side of neck edge every other row 3 (3, 4) times. Work on 14 (15, 16) sts each side until armhole measures 4¼ (4½, 4¾) inches.

Shape Shoulder: At arm edge bind off 7 (7, 8) sts once and 7 (8, 8) sts once.

SWEATER BACK (Right Side): With smaller needles, cast on 29 (31, 33) sts.

Row 1: K 3 for border, *p 1, k 1, repeat from * in ribbing to end of row.

Row 2: P 1, k 1 in ribbing to last 3 sts, k 3 for border.

Repeat Rows 1 and 2 for 7 more rows. Change to larger needles.

Work in stockinette (k 1 row, p 1 row) continuing 3 st border in garter st until piece measures 7½ (8, 8½) inches, end with p row.

Shape armhole in same manner as front and work until armhole measures 4¼ (4½, 4¾) inches, end with p row—26 (27, 29) sts on needle.

Shape Shoulders: At arm edge bind off 7 (7, 8) sts once and 7 (8, 8) sts once. Sl remaining 12 (12, 13) sts onto holder.

SWEATER BACK (Left Side): Work to correspond to right side, reversing placement of shaping and border.

Sew front and back shoulder seams together.

HOOD (Right Side): With smaller needles pick up 9 (9, 11) sts along neck edge of right side of front, sl sts from holder for right side of back onto needle and k across these sts. Keep the 3 sts at center back edge in garter st. Work in ribbing of k 1, p 1 for 7 (7, 9) rows, ending on wrong side of work. Change to larger needles. K 5 sts, inc 6 sts evenly across row. Work in stockinette, inc one st inside garter st every ½ inch 3 times. Work even for 6 (6½, 6¾) inches above ribbing, end with k row. Bind off 3 garter sts and work 3 more rows in stockinette. Sl these sts onto holder.

Left Side: Work to correspond to right side.

Weave sts from holders together for top of hood.

SLEEVES: With smaller needles, cast on 33 (37, 39) sts.

Row 1: Work in k 1, p 1 ribbing for 9 rows. Change to larger needles and work in stockinette, inc one st each end of needle every inch 5 times. Work on 43 (47, 49) sts until piece measures 7½ (8¼, 9½) or desired inches.

Shape Cap: At beginning of each of next 2 rows bind off 2 sts. Dec one st each end of needle every other row for 2¾ (3, 3¼) inches. At beginning of each of next 6 rows, bind off 2 sts. Bind off remaining sts.

Finishing: With double pointed needles, pick up 111 (113, 117) sts around front edge of hood, sl 17 sts from holder at center front onto needle and k across these sts. Divide sts evenly on three needles and work in k 1, p 1 ribbing for 14 rounds. Bind off loosely in ribbing. Fold ribbing double to wrong side and sew loosely to front edge of hood. Sew zipper in place under garter sts with open end of zipper placed at waist end. With black yarn or thread, sew buttons in place for owl's eyes. Sew in sleeves. Sew side seam and sleeve seam. If desired, elastic thread may be run through ribbing around front edge of hood to prevent stretching.

Pompom: Wind yarn around a 1½ inch piece of cardboard 35 times. Slip yarn from cardboard and tie securely at center leaving long ends to sew pompom in place. Clip each end and trim evenly. Sew pompom to hood at top of garter sts.

LEGGINGS (Right Half): With smaller needles, cast on 72 (74, 76) sts for waist facing.

Rows 1 through 4: Work in stockinette.

Row 5: K each st on p side for turning ridge.

Rows 6 through 10: Work in stockinette, ending with a k row.

Change to larger needles and p 1 row.

Begin short rows for back shaping. First and 2nd Short Rows—k 8, turn, sl one st, p 7.

Third and 4th Short Rows: K 7, with right needle, pick up st directly below sl st and sl it to left needle, work this st tog with sl st to prevent hole in work. K 8, turn, sl 1, p 15. Always work sl as before. Continue to work 8 sts more every k row until there are 40 sts worked. On next k row, work all sts.

Continue stockinette, inc one st each side every 2 inches 3 (3, 4) times—78 (80, 84) sts. Work even until 9 (9½, 10) or desired inches above turning edge, measured at short edge, end with p row. Dec one st each side of next row. Repeat dec every second row 4 (4, 5) times; every 6th row 7 (7, 8) times—54 (56, 56) sts. Work even until 16 (18, 20½) or desired inches from turning edge.

Dec Row: *Work first 2 sts tog, work 2 sts, repeat from * across row, ending k 2 tog—40 (42, 42) sts. With smaller needles, work k 1, p 1 in ribbing for 2½ inches. Bind off loosely in ribbing.

LEGGINGS (Left Half): Work to correspond to right half. Change to larger needles to k row 10.

First and 2nd Short Rows: P 8, turn, sl 1, k 7.

Continue short rows to correspond to right half, purling 8 sts more every second row, working slipped sts as in right half. Continue to work as for right half.

Finishing: Sew seams together. Fold along turning edge and sew hem loosely around waist; insert elastic. Make elastic straps to fit from cuff ribbing over soles of shoes.

RIGHT MITTEN (Cuff): With number 3 (5, 5) needles, cast on 32 sts. Work k 1, p 1 ribbing for 2 inches, dec one st in last row—31 sts.

Hand (Pattern Rows and Thumb Gore): Row 1: K 3, p 1, k 8, p 1, k 18.

Row 2: P 18, k 1, p 8, k 1, p 3.

Row 3: (Begin Owl) K 3, p 10 for owl sts, k 18.

Note: Work owl same as on sweater front, making twists on Rows 7, 17 and 23.

Row 4: Repeat Row 2.

Row 5: (Thumb Inc) K 3, p 1, k 8, p 1, k 2, place marker, inc one st in next st (first thumb st), k 1, inc one st in next st (last thumb st), place marker, k 13 sts.

Row 6: P 20, (slip thumb markers each row), k 1, p 8, k 1, p 3.

Rows 7 through 12: Work thumb inc on Rows 7, 9 and 11 and begin owl on Row 7. Thumb Inc: Inc one st in first and last thumb sts and k the sts between inc.

Row 13: (Dividing Row—Right Side) K 3, p 1, k 8, p 1, k 2, sl these 15 sts onto holder for back of hand, k 11 sts for thumb, sl remaining 13 sts onto another holder for palm.

Thumb: Turn, p thumb sts, cast on 2 sts loosely. Continue in stockinette on 13 sts until thumb measures ¾ (1, 1¼) inches above cast on sts, end with p row, dec one st in last row.

First Dec Row: (*K 1, k 2 tog) 4 times. P 1 row. K 2 tog 4 times. Fasten off, leaving an end. Draw end tightly through all sts. Fasten securely. Sew thumb seam.

Sl sts for back of hand from holder onto needle, join yarn in last st, pick up and k 2 sts on cast on thumb sts, sl sts for palm of hand from holder onto another needle and k across—30 sts on needle. Continue to work in pattern with owl twists on Rows 17 and 23 until measurement above cuff is 3 (3½, 3¾) or desired inches. Allow ½ inch for finishing, end with p row, dec 2 sts in last row.

First Dec Row: (K 2, k 2 tog) 7 times. P next row.

Second Dec Row: (K 1, k 2 tog) 7 times. P next row. K 2 tog 7 times. Finish as for thumb. Sew eyes in place on owls, sew side seams.

Left Mitten: Work same as right mitten, but place owl on opposite side of mitten. Row 1 after ribbing: K 18, (p 1, k 8, p 1 for owl), k 3. Continue in same manner as right mitten.

Make a chain 30 inches long (or suitable length) and sew end of cord to each mitten cuff.

CHILD'S "CHOO CHOO" CARDIGAN

Intermediate—Challenging

The **traditional favorite steam** engine chugs along with puffs of pompom smoke on this adorable sweater. Directions are given for size 2 with changes for sizes 4, 6 and 8 in parentheses. You will need 6 (8, 8, 10) ounces red knitting worsted, 1 ounce black knitting worsted, one pair each numbers 5 and 8 knitting needles (or size needed to work to gauge), size 0 steel crochet hook, 6 buttons for front

closing and 2 small ⅝ inch and 1 large 1⅛ inch dark buttons for train wheels.

Gauge: 5 sts equal 1 inch
6 rows equal 1 inch

BACK: With red, using smaller needles, cast on 56 (60, 64, 68) sts. Work in ribbing (k 1, p 1) for 2 inches. Change to larger needles and work even in stockinette until piece measures 8 (9, 10, 11) inches, ending with a p row. Cut yarn and place sts on holder.

LEFT FRONT: With red using smaller needles, cast on 28 (30, 32, 34) sts. Work in ribbing for 2 inches. Change to larger needles, work in stockinette for 4 rows. Using black for train, work from chart for next 19 rows. Fasten off black yarn. Continue working stockinette with red until piece measures 8 (9, 10, 11) inches, end with p row. Cut yarn and place sts on st holder.

RIGHT FRONT: With red, work in same manner as for left front, omitting train. Do not cut yarn, place sts on holder.

SLEEVE: Using smaller needles and red yarn, cast on 34 (36, 36, 38) sts. Work in ribbing for 2 inches. Change to larger needles and work in stockinette, inc one st at beginning and end of needle every 1¼ inches 5 (6, 7, 8) times. Work even on 44 (48, 50, 54) sts until piece measures 9½ (10½, 11½, 12½) inches, ending with a p row. Cut yarn and place sts on holder. Make a second sleeve in same manner.

To Join for Raglan Shaping: Row 1: K 28 (30, 32, 34) sts of right front, put a marker on needle, k 44 (48, 50, 54) sts of one sleeve, put a marker on needle, k 56 (60, 64, 68) sts of back, put a marker on needle, k 44 (48, 50, 54) sts of other sleeve, put a marker on needle, k 28 (30, 32, 34) sts of left front—200 (216, 228, 244) sts.

Row 2: P.

Row 3: *K to 3 sts before next marker, k 2 tog (dec), k 1, sl 1, k 1, psso (dec), repeat from * 3 times, k to end of row—8 sts dec.

Repeat last 2 rows 9 (11, 12, 14) times, end with Row 2—120 (120, 124, 124) sts.

Shape Neck: Continue to dec one st each side of marker on every k row 8 times. AT THE SAME TIME, bind off 4 (4, 5, 5) sts at beginning of each of next 2 rows, then dec one st at beginning and end of needle every other row 4 times. Work until all raglan dec have been completed and there are 36 (36,

38, 38) sts on needle. P 1 row. Cut yarn.

Neck Ribbing: With right side facing using smaller needles and red yarn, pick up and k 14 sts along right front, k 36 sts of back from larger needle, pick up and k 14 sts along left front. Work in ribbing for 7 rows. Bind off loosely in ribbing.

Finishing: Sew or crochet underarm and sleeve seams.

Left Front Band for Boys: Using red with right side facing, work 2 rows of sc on left front edge.

Row 3: (Buttonholes) Work sc in each of next 2 sc, ch 2, sk 2 sc, sc in each sc in next buttonhole. Make 5 more buttonholes evenly spaced; the last buttonhole should be ½ inch above bottom edge.

Right Front Band for Boys: With red, work 3 rows of sc along right front edge.

For Girls: Make as for boys except buttonholes should be on right front.

Block. Sew buttons in place.

Coverings for ⅝ inch Buttons: With black and smaller needles, cast on 6 sts. Work in stockinette for 2 rows.

Next Row: Inc one st at beginning and end of piece (8 sts). Work 2 rows in stockinette.

Next Row: Dec one st at beginning and end of row (6 sts). Work 2 rows even. Bind off. Cut yarn, leaving a length of yarn. Thread end into tapestry needle, run yarn around edge, pull snugly together over button, fasten securely on back of button. Sew to lower front edge of engine to form wheel. Whip outer edge of wheel button to sweater. Make a second button in same manner and sew next to first button.

Large Button Covering: Cast on 8 sts. Work in stockinette for 2 rows.

Next Row: K each st, inc one st at beginning and end of row (10 sts).

P 1 row.

Next Row: K each st, inc one st at beginning and end of row (12 sts).

Work 3 rows even.

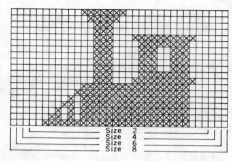

Next Row: Continue stockinette st, dec one st at beginning and end of row (10 sts).

P 1 row. Repeat dec row (8 sts). Work 2 rows even.

Bind off and finish as for ⅝ inch buttons. Sew in place at lower back edge of engine.

Pompoms: With white yarn, make 2 small pompoms. Sew to sweater for smoke. To make pompoms: Wind 20 strands of yarn over a 2 inch cardboard, tie around center, cut ends and trim into a ball.

CHILD'S "GROW" SWEATER

Intermediate

Sweater is knit from the neck down and, as child grows, ribbing can be unraveled for more length in stockinette, with reserved yarn added in ribbing. Directions are for size 4 with any changes for sizes 6, 8, 10, 12 and 14 in parentheses. You need about 12 (12, 12, 16, 16, 16) ounces royal blue and one ounce each red, yellow and green 4-ply knitting worsted weight yarn, one pair each numbers 5 and 8 standard knitting needles and one set double pointed needles number 5.

Gauge: 5 sts equal 1 inch
6 rows equal 1 inch

BACK: Begin at neck, with larger needles, cast on 20 (20, 20, 24, 24, 26) sts.

Rows 1, 3: P.

Row 2: K 1, inc one st in next st, k to last 2 sts, inc one st in next st, k 1.

Work in stockinette (k 1 row, p 1 row), inc 2 sts every k row until 19 (21, 24, 25, 27, 29) inc have been made—58 (62, 68, 74, 78, 84) sts on needle.

Armhole: Cast on 2 sts at end of each of next 2 rows—62 (66, 72, 78, 82, 88) sts.

Work in stockinette until piece measures 5 (5½, 6, 6½, 7, 7½) or desired inches below armhole. End on wrong side row.

Stripe Pattern Rows: Joining and changing colors, work 4 red rows, 1 blue row, 4 yellow rows, 1 blue row, 4 green rows.

Work 3 rows in blue in stockinette. Change to smaller needles and work 1 row.

K 1, p 1 across each row in ribbing for 2½ inches. Bind sts off loosely in ribbing.

FRONTS: With larger needles, cast on 2 sts for one front, drop yarn. With another skein to be used (until otherwise specified) for other front, cast on 2 sts—2 sts for **each** front.

Rows 1,3: P each st with its own yarn.

Row 2: K 1, inc one st in next st (neck edge), drop yarn. Inc one st in st of other front (neck edge), k 1.

Row 4: Inc one st in first st (arm edge), k to last st, inc one st for neck, drop yarn. Inc one st each end of other front.

Working in stockinette, inc one st at each neck and arm edge every k row until each front has 9 (9, 9, 11, 11, 13) sts.

Joining: P across one front, then **with same yarn,** cast on 12 (12, 12, 14, 14, 14) sts and p across other front, fasten off unused skein.

Continue working raglan inc same as back until there are 58 (62, 68, 74, 78, 84) sts. Cast on 2 sts at each armhole and work front same as back.

SLEEVES: With larger needles, cast on 8 (8, 4, 4, 4, 4) sts.

Inc one st each end for raglan on k rows same as for back until 46 (50, 52, 54, 58, 62) sts on needle. Cast on 2 sts each end on next 2 rows for armhole and dec one st each end of needle every inch until there are 36 (36, 40, 40, 44, 44) sts and AT SAME TIME when sleeve is 5½ (6½, 7, 7½, 8, 8½) inches, work stripes.

Change to smaller needles and p 1 row. Work 3 inches ribbing. Bind off loosely in ribbing.

Finishing: Sew sleeves. Right side facing, with double pointed needles, pick up and k an even number of sts around neck. Work k 1, p 1 ribbing for 4½ (4½, 4½, 5, 5, 5) inches. Bind off loosely.

CHILD'S "HELLO" CARDIGAN

Intermediate-Challenging

This basic raglan sweater can be made in one color or several colors. The model was made of knitting worsted in light gray (MC), dark gray (A), red (B) and white (C). Directions are given for size 4 with changes in parentheses for sizes 6, 8 and 10. Materials needed are 6 (8, 10, 10) ounces knitting worsted for MC, 2 (2, 3, 4) ounces for color A, 1 (1, 2, 2) ounces for color B, small amount for color C, one pair each numbers 5 and 8 standard knitting needles, a number 0 steel crochet hook and 6 buttons.

Gauge: 5 sts equal 1 inch
6 rows equal 1 inch

BACK: Using smaller needles and B, cast on 60 (64, 68, 74) sts.

Work in ribbing of k 1, p 1 for 2 rows. Change to A and continue in ribbing until piece measures 2 inches.

Change to larger needles and MC and work even in stockinette st for 2 rows. Work next 18 rows in stockinette st following chart. Work even with MC until piece measures 10 inches, ending with a p row. Fasten off and sl sts onto st holder.

LEFT FRONT: Using smaller needles and B, cast on 30 (32, 34, 36) sts.

Work in ribbing of k 1, p 1 for 2 rows. Change to A and continue in ribbing until piece measures 2 inches.

Change to larger needles and MC and work even in stockinette st until piece measures 10 inches, ending with p row. Fasten off and sl sts onto st holder.

RIGHT FRONT: Work same as left front, reversing shaping. Do not fasten off yarn.

SLEEVES: (Make 2) Using smaller needles and B, cast on 36 (36, 38, 40) sts.

Work in ribbing of k 1, p 1 for 2 rows. Change to A and continue in ribbing until piece measures 2 inches.

Change to larger needles and MC and work in stockinette st, inc one st each end of needle every 1 inch 6 (7, 8, 9) times. Work even on 48 (50, 54, 58)

sts until piece measures 10½ (11½, 12½, 13½) inches, ending with p row. Fasten off and sl sts onto st holder.

To Join for Raglan Shaping: Row 1: K 30 (32, 34, 36) sts of right front, place marker on needle, k 48 (50, 54, 58) sts of one sleeve, place marker on needle, k 60 (64, 68, 74) sts of back, place marker on needle, k 48 (50, 54, 58) sts of other sleeve, place marker on needle, k 30 (32, 34, 36) sts of left front—216 (228, 244, 262) sts.

Row 2: P.

Row 3: *K to 3 sts before next marker, k 2 tog, k 1, sl marker, sl 1, k 1, psso, repeat from * 3 times more, k to end of row—8 sts dec.

Repeat last 2 rows 11 (12, 14, 16) times more, ending with Row 2—120 (124, 124, 126) sts.

Shape Neck: Continue to dec one st each side of each marker on every k row 8 times more and AT SAME TIME at beginning of each of next 2 rows bind off 4 (5, 5, 5) sts. At beginning of each of next 2 rows bind off 2 sts and then dec one st each end of needle every other row 4 times. Work until all raglan dec have been completed and there are 36 (38, 38 40) sts on needle. P 1 row.

Neck Ribbing: With right side facing and using smaller needles and A, pick up and k 14 sts along right front, k 36 (38, 38, 40) sts from larger needle, pick up and k 14 sts along left front.

Work in ribbing of k 1, p 1 on 64 (66, 66, 68) sts for 5 (5, 7, 7) rows. Change to B and continue in ribbing for 2 rows more. Bind off.

Finishing: Sew underarm and sleeve seams.

Left Front Band for Boys: Using A with right side facing, work 2 rows sc on left front edge.

Row 3: (Buttonhole Row) Work 2 sc, ch 2, sk 2 sc, sc in next sc. Make 5 more buttonholes evenly spaced, the last one ½ inch above lower edge.

Right Front Band for Boys: Work 3 rows sc along edge of right front.

For girls work buttonholes on right front edge, first one ½ inch above lower edge and last one ½ inch below neck edge.

Embroider faces in letters as shown, using C. Block. Sew on buttons.

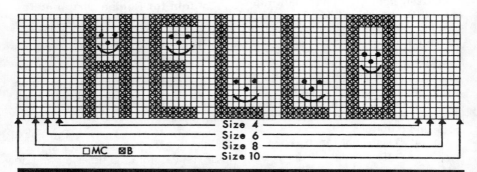

□ MC   ⊠ B

Size 4
Size 6
Size 8
Size 10

BOY'S CARDIGAN, CAP & MITTEN SET

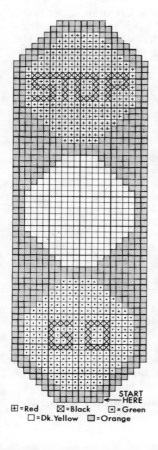

⊞ = Red   ⊠ = Black   ⊡ = Green
□ = Dk. Yellow   ⊞ = Orange

START HERE →

Challenging

Stop **a moment** and look at this sweater that will take your youngster wherever he wants to **go.** Directions are for size 4 with any changes for sizes 6 and 8 in parentheses. Boy's set requires about 12 (12, 16) ounces pale yellow knitting worsted weight yarn and 1 ounce each orange, red, green and dark yellow and small amount black. Use one pair each numbers 5 and 8 standard knitting needles and one set number 5 double pointed needles.

Gauge: 5 sts equal 1 inch
7 rows equal 1 inch

CARDIGAN
BACK: With smaller needles and yellow, cast on 63 (67, 73) sts.

Row 1: (K 1, p 1) across row, ending with k 1. Continue in ribbing for 1½ inches.

With larger needles, work in stockinette (k 1 row, p 1 row) until back is 10 (10½, 11) inches.

Armhole and Raglan Shaping: Bind off 2 sts at beginning of next 2 rows.

Row 1: K 1, k 2 tog, k to last 3 sts, sl 1, k 1, psso, k 1.

Row 2: P.

Repeat last 2 rows until 21 sts remain; sl to holder for back of neck.

LEFT FRONT: With smaller needles and yellow, cast on 36 (38, 42) sts.

Row 1: (Wrong Side) K 1, p 4, k 1 (border sts), (p 1, k 1) across row.

Row 2: Work ribbing to last 6 sts, k 6 sts (border sts).

Repeat last 2 rows for 1½ inches, ending with wrong side row.

With larger needles, work 2 rows stockinette, keeping border sts in pattern as established.

Next Row: (Begin Chart) K 12 (13, 15) sts, join orange and work first 8 sts of chart, join another strand yellow, k last 16 (17, 19) sts. **Note:** Work black sts on green light, work red light in **solid** red (no black).

Continue working from chart and when front is same as back to armhole, bind off 2 sts at beginning of next k

side row.

Work 1 row even.

Row 1: K 1, k 2 tog, k across.

Row 2: K 1, p 4, k 1, p across.

Repeat last two rows continuing to work chart until 10 (12, 15) arm dec have been made.

Neck Shaping: At neck edge, p 8 sts and sl to holder, p across. Dec 1 st at neck edge every k row 7 (7, 8) times, and AT SAME TIME continue raglan dec. Bind off last st.

RIGHT FRONT: With smaller needles and yellow, cast on 36 (38, 42) sts.

Row 1: (Wrong Side) (K 1, p 1), repeat across row to last 6 sts, k 1, p 4, k 1.

Row 2: K 6, (k 1, p 1) in ribbing across.

Work for 1½ inches ribbing, end with a wrong side row.

With larger needles and keeping border as established, work 2 rows stockinette.

Next Row: (Begin Chart) K 16 (17, 19) sts, joining yarns, work first 8 sts of chart and k last 12 (13, 15) sts. **Note:** Work green light in **solid** green and work black sts on red light only.

Work to correspond to left front, reversing placement of shapings and working raglan same as left arm edge of back.

SLEEVES: With smaller needles and yellow, cast on 36 (36, 40) sts.

(K 1, p 1) in ribbing for 2½ inches.

With larger needles, work in stockinette, inc one st each end of needle every inch 7 (9, 8) times—50 (54, 56) sts.

Continue in stockinette until sleeve is 11 (12, 12½) or desired inches to armhole.

Shape Raglan Armhole: Bind off 2 sts at beginning of next 2 rows. Work raglan same as back until there are 8 (8, 4) sts to sl to holder.

Finishing: Set in raglan sleeves to back and front. Sew underarm and sleeve seams.

Neckband: On right side of work, pick up and k 65 or an odd number of sts around neck edge, including all sts from holders and along neck shapings.

Work border sts as established and work p 1, k 1 ribbing on other sts for 2½ inches. Bind off.

Fold neck ribbing double and loosely sew in place to wrong side. Block, being careful not to stretch. Sew ribbon to wrong side of each front border. Work 5 machine buttonholes evenly spaced on left front. Sew buttons to right front.

CAP: (One size fits all) With smaller standard needles and yellow, cast on 108 sts.

K 1, p 1 in ribbing for 4 inches, fasten off.

With larger needles and joining each new color, k 9 orange sts, k 27 green sts, k 9 orange sts, k 27 yellow, k 9 orange sts, k 27 red sts.

Work each st in its own color in stockinette for 17 rows. Fasten off each strand.

Join yellow and p across to last 2 sts, p 2 tog.

Dec Row: With smaller needles, (k 2, k 2 tog), repeat across row—80 sts.

Work k 1, p 1 ribbing for 6 rows.

Repeat dec row—60 sts.

Work 5 rows ribbing.

(K 2 tog) across row—30 sts.

P 1 row.

(K 3 tog) across row—10 sts.

Leave end, thread tapestry needle and draw through the 10 sts.

Draw up tight and fasten securely. Sew center back seam. Block.

Make pompom and sew to top of cap.

Pompom: Wind yarn around a 1½ inch piece of cardboard 35 times. Slip yarn from cardboard and tie securely at center leaving long ends for sewing onto cap. Trim even.

MITTENS: Directions are for size 4 with sizes 6 and 8 in parentheses.

RIGHT MITTEN: Cuff: With smaller needles and yellow, cast on 32 (36, 40) sts.

K 1, p 1 in ribbing for 2½ (2¾, 3) inches, dec 0 (1, 1) st in last row—32 (35, 39) sts.

Hand: Beginning with k row, work stockinette for 4 rows.

Thumb Gore: K 15 (17, 19) sts, inc one st in next st (first thumb st), k 1, inc one st in next st (last thumb st), k remaining 14 (15, 17) sts.

P 1 row.

K 15 (17, 19) sts, inc one st in next st, k 3, inc one st in next st, k remaining 14 (15, 17) sts—36 (39, 43) sts on needle.

Continue to inc one st in first and last thumb sts every k row, having 2 more sts between inc after each inc row. Inc 2 (2, 3) times more.

Work even for 3 (3, 5) rows on 40 (43, 49) sts.

Dividing Row: K 15 (17, 19) sts and sl to holder for back of hand. K 11 (11, 13) thumb sts onto a double pointed needle and cast on one st at end of thumb sts, sl remaining 14 (15, 17) sts onto holder for palm.

Thumb: Divide thumb sts on 3 needles (the needle with the cast on st will be the last needle of each rnd).

K 9 (11, 13) rnds on 12 (12, 14) sts.

First Dec Row: (K 1, k 2 tog), repeat around, end k 0 (0, 2).

K 1 rnd.

Next Rnd: (K 2 tog), repeat around. Fasten off, leaving an end. Draw end tightly through all sts and fasten securely. Sl sts for back of hand onto standard needle, join yarn in last st, pick up and k one st in cast on st, sl sts from holder for palm onto standard needle and k these sts—30 (33, 37) sts on needle.

P 1 row, k 1 row, p 1 row, fasten off.

With red, k 1 row, p 1 row. Work other sts in red, work black sts for STOP from chart, centering lettering on back of hand sts. Complete letters, fasten off black, and work 2 more rows of red, fasten off red. Join yellow and work until measurement is 4 (5, 5½) or desired inches above cuff, allowing ½ inch for finishing. End with p row.

Dec Row: (K 2, k 2 tog), repeat across row, end k 2 (1, 1).

P 1 row.

(K 1, k 2 tog), repeat across row, end k 2 (1, 1).

P 1 row.

(K 2 tog), repeat across row, end k 0 (1, 1).

Finish as for thumb and sew side seam. Work in ends and block.

LEFT MITTEN: Work same as for right mitten to first inc row.

Thumb Gore: K 14 (15, 17) sts for palm, inc one st in next st (first thumb st), k 1, inc one st in next st (last thumb st), k 15 (17, 19) sts for back of hand. Continue to work to correspond to right mitten, fasten off yellow, join green in place of red and work the lettering GO from chart on back of hand.

MAN'S PULLOVER SWEATER
Intermediate

This sleek, smooth pullover is sure to appeal to the man in your life! Directions are given for size 38 with changes for sizes 40, 42 and 44 in parentheses. You will need the following amounts of 4-ply fingering yarn in desired color: 15 (16, 17, 18) ounces. Use standard knitting needles numbers 2 and 3 and a set of number 2 double pointed needles or size needles needed to work to gauge.

Measurements: Length from back of neck 25 (25½, 26, 26½) inches
To fit chest measurement of 38 (40, 42, 44) inches.
Sleeve Seam: 18 (18, 19, 19) inches.
Gauge: 7½ sts equal 1 inch
9½ rows equal 1 inch

BACK: Using smaller needles, cast on 150 (158, 166, 174) sts and work 3 inches in k 1, p 1 ribbing. Change to larger needles and stockinette st and continue until work measures 15 inches or desired length from beginning to underarm, ending with a p row.
Raglan Shaping: Bind off 7 (7, 8, 8) sts at beginning of next 2 rows.
Row 3: K 2 tog, k to last 2 sts, sl 1, k 1, psso.
Row 4: P.
Repeat Rows 3 and 4 until 46 (48, 50, 50) sts remain, ending with a p row. Place remaining sts on stitch holder for neckband.

FRONT: Using smaller needles, cast on 150 (158, 166, 174) sts and work 3 inches in k 1, p 1 ribbing, inc one st on last rib row—151 (159, 167, 175) sts on needle. Change to larger needles, work same as back until there are 133 (141, 147, 155) sts on needle, ending with a k row. Divide sts for neck opening.

Next Row: P 66 (70, 73, 77), sl next st onto st holder for neckband, p to end. Working both sides at once, continue raglan shaping as before and AT SAME TIME dec one st at neck edge on next row and every 4th row 21 (22, 23, 23) times in all. Continue raglan shaping until 2 sts remain, ending with a p row. K 2 tog, fasten off.

SLEEVES: Using smaller needles, cast on 66 (70, 72, 76) sts and work 3 inches in k 1, p 1 ribbing. Change to larger needles and stockinette st, inc one st at each end of 5th row, then every 4th row until there are 74 (84, 88, 98) sts on needle, then every 6th row until there are 112 (118, 124, 130) sts on needle. Continue without further shaping until work measures 18 (18, 19, 19) inches or desired length from beginning to underarm, ending with a p row.
Raglan Shaping: Bind off 7 (7, 8, 8) sts at beginning of next 2 rows.
Next Row: K.
Next Row: P.
Next Row: K 2 tog, k to last 2 sts, sl 1, k 1, psso.
Next Row: P.
Repeat these 4 rows until 90 (96, 100, 104) st remain, ending with a p row, then work same as raglan shaping for back until 16 sts remain, ending with a p row. Place remaining sts on st holder for neckband.

Finishing: Press lightly under warm iron and damp cloth. Join raglan seams, sew side and sleeve seams.

Neckband: With right side of work facing you, place back and left sleeve sts from st holders onto smaller needles, pick up and k 76 sts along left neck edge, place a marker on needle, pick up center front st, place a marker on needle, pick up and k 75 sts along right front edge, pick up sts from right sleeve st holder. Arrange 230 (232, 234, 234) sts on 3 needles. With 4th needle work in rnds of k 1, p 1 ribbing for 1 inch, always k center st and dec one st before first marker and after second marker every alternate rnd. Bind off loosely in ribbing.

WOMAN'S PULLOVER SWEATER

Challenging

This pullover ski sweater with Indian designs will look great on the slopes or by the fireplace. Directions are given for size 10 with sizes 12, 14 and 16 in parentheses. Materials required are about 16 (16, 20, 20) ounces of off-white 4-ply knitting worsted weight yarn, small amounts of coral, turquoise and black yarn, standard knitting needles numbers 5 and 8, one set number 5 double pointed needles or size to obtain gauge, crochet hook and bobbins.

Gauge: 5 sts equal 1 inch
7 rows equal 1 inch

BACK: With smaller needles, cast on 85 (89, 93, 97) sts. Work in ribbing as follows:

Row 1: K 1, *p 1, k 1, repeat from * to end of row.

Row 2: P 1, *k 1, p 1, repeat from * to end of row.

Repeat Rows 1 and 2 for 3½ inches. Change to larger needles. Work 6 rows in stockinette (k 1 row, p 1 row), then work lightning pattern from graph and continue in stockinette with main color after completing pattern.

Note: The Crossed Arrows mean "Friendship," the Thunderbird, "Sacred Bearer of Happiness Unlimited," the Butterfly, "Everlasting Life."

Work until piece measures 12 (12½, 13, 13½) inches or desired length to armhole.

Raglan Shaping: Bind off 2 sts at beginning of next 2 rows. Work raglan dec as follows:

Row 1: K 1, k 2 tog, k to last 3 sts, sl 1, k 1, psso, k 1.

Row 2: P.

After 6 (7, 9, 12) dec have been worked, work in pattern from graph for butterflies and thunderbird, centering thunderbird on the 13 center sts, the butterflies 4 sts on either side of thunderbird. Complete pattern from

graph, continue working raglan dec until total of 28 (29, 31, 34) dec have been made. Sl remaining 25 (27, 27, 25) sts onto holder for back of neck.

FRONT: Work exactly same as back until 20 (21, 23, 26) dec have been made—41 (43, 43, 41) sts on needle.

Continue raglan dec and sl center 17 (19, 19, 17) sts onto holder for center front, work across remaining sts. Join another skein of yarn and work both sides of front at same time. Dec one st each side of neck edge every k row 4 (4, 4, 4) times. Continue raglan dec until no sts are left.

SLEEVES: With smaller needles, cast on 41 (41, 45, 49) sts. Work ribbing same as on back for 3 inches, inc 8 sts evenly spaced on last row. Change to larger needles, work 6 rows in stockinette. Work lightning pattern from graph same as on back and front pieces. After graph is completed, inc one st each end of needle every inch 7 (9, 9, 8) times—63 (67, 71, 73) sts on needle. Continue to work in stockinette until sleeve measures 16½ (17, 17½, 18) inches or desired length.

Raglan Shaping: Bind off 2 sts at beginning of next 2 rows. Work raglan dec same as on back until 5 (6, 8, 11) dec have been made. Work from graph and center crossed arrows on sleeve, continue to work raglan dec until 28 (29, 31, 34) dec have been made. Sl remaining 5 (7, 7, 3) sts onto holder.

Finishing: Sew sleeves to back and front pieces. Sew sleeve and side seams. With double pointed needles, right side facing, pick up and k approximately 76 (82, 82, 82) sts around neck edge including sts from all holders. K 1, p 1 in ribbing for 5 inches. Bind sts off loosely in ribbing. Fold ribbing over for turtle neck. Knot fringe in every other st using 2 strands of yarn. Trim fringe evenly (approximately 1 inch in length). Work in ends and block.

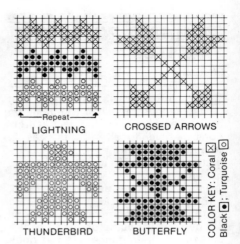

LIGHTNING   CROSSED ARROWS

THUNDERBIRD   BUTTERFLY

COLOR KEY: Coral ⊠
Black ● ; Turquoise ○

WOMAN'S RAGLAN-SLEEVE CARDIGAN

Challenging

This original raglan sweater design features no seams. A lovely maple leaf pattern and stockinette stitch are combined for a simple yet elegant sweater. Directions are given for size 12 with changes in parentheses for sizes 14 and 16. Materials needed are 16 ounces knitting worsted (all sizes), one pair number 4 knitting needles, a number 8 circular knitting needle, one set each numbers 4 and 8 double pointed knitting needles or sizes to give gauge, size 00 crochet hook and 6 buttons.

Gauge: 4½ sts equal 1 inch
6 rows equal 1 inch

Pattern Stitch: (Worked on 9 sts for front bands and raglan seams)

Row 1 and All Odd Rows: P.

Row 2: K 2 tog, yo, k 1, yo, sl 1, k 2 tog, psso, yo, k 1, yo, sl 1, k 1, psso.

Row 4: K 2 tog, yo, k 5, yo, sl 1, k 1, psso.

Row 6: Repeat Row 4.

Row 8: K 2, yo, sl 1, k 1, psso, k 1, k 2 tog, yo, k 2.

Repeat these 8 rows for pattern.

Beginning at neck with smaller

straight needles, cast on 79 sts (all sizes). Work in k 1, p 1 ribbing for 7 rows. Change to circular needle.

Row 1: (Wrong Side) P 9, place marker, p 1, place marker, p 9, place marker, p 3, place marker, p 9, place marker, p 17, place marker, p 9, place marker, p 3, place marker, p 9, place marker, p 1, place marker, p 9.

Row 2: Beginning with Row 2 of pattern and slipping all markers, work pattern at each front and at each raglan seam as follows: Work pattern on first 9 sts, inc one st in next st, pattern on next 9 sts, inc one st in next st, k 1, inc one st in next st, pattern on next 9 sts, inc one st in next st, k 15, inc one st in next st, pattern on next 9 sts, inc one st in next st, k 1, inc one st in next st, pattern on next 9 sts, inc one st in next st, work pattern on last 9 sts.

Row 3 and All Odd Rows: P.

Continue in established pattern, inc before and after each raglan seam pattern (8 incs on each k row) until there are 27 (29, 31) inc rows or 295 (311, 327) sts, ending with p row.

BODY: (Dividing Row) Do not make raglan inc or pattern at raglan seams on this row but DO continue patterns at front edges. Working across left front (keeping first 9 sts in pattern), k 42 (44, 46) sts, k next 65 (69, 73) sts and place on holder to be worked later for left sleeve, k next 81 (85, 89) sts for back, k next 65 (69, 73) sts and place on holder to be worked later for right sleeve, k next 42 (44, 46) sts for right front (keeping last 9 sts in pattern)—165 (173, 181) sts.

Next Row: (Wrong Side) Work across in established pattern, casting on 2 sts at underarms, making 169 (177, 185) sts for body.

Continue until work measures 8 inches from underarms. Change to smaller straight needles and work in k 1, p 1 ribbing for 2 inches. Bind off in ribbing.

SLEEVES: With larger double pointed needles and right side facing, pick up and k sleeve sts from holder, divide sts on 3 needles, pick up and k 2

sts at underarm (place marker between these 2 sts). K each rnd, dec 2 sts every 2 inches 4 times by k 2 tog on each side of marker. Work even until sleeve measures 10 inches from underarm. Change to smaller double pointed needles and work in k 1, p 1 ribbing for 2 inches. Bind off in ribbing. Make second sleeve to correspond.

Bands: With size 00 crochet hook and starting at lower right front, join yarn and sc 67 sts to neck edge, turn, sc in each st across, turn.

Buttonhole Row: Sc in first 3 sc, *ch 2, sk 2, sc in next 10 sc, repeat from * to neck, sc in remaining sts, turn. Work 2 more rows sc. Repeat for other front, omitting buttonholes. Sew buttons in position. Block to size.

LOUNGING SLIPPERS

Intermediate

These comfortable slippers utilize straight, circular and double pointed needles. Directions are given for women's size with men's sizes in parentheses. You need about 4 ounces black, 4 ounces orange 4-ply knitting worsted weight yarn, 1 pair number 6 standard knitting needles, a number 6 circular needle (14 inches or shorter), 1 set number 6 double pointed needles; yarn needle.

Gauge: 5 sts equal 1 inch

Sole: With black and straight needles, cast on 86 (96) sts. Work 16 rows garter st (k each row). For wider feet, k 18 or 20 rows.

Body of Sock: Next Row: Change to circular needle (or divide stitches evenly on double pointed needles and work in rounds). With black, k 40 (45), k 2 tog, p 2, k 2 tog in back of sts, k 40 (45). Place marker on needle. Continue working around in circular fashion.

Row 2: K 39 (44), k 2 tog, p 2, k 2 tog in back of sts, k 39 (44).

Row 3: K 38 (43), k 2 tog, p 2, k 2 tog in back of sts, k 38 (43).

Work each row, dec one st before and after the p 2 sts until 40 sts remain.

Pattern: Row 4: Join orange. Begin working pattern from chart right to left to two center purl sts.

Note: All k 2 tog sts should be knitted in orange; all p 2 sts in black, even if this doesn't follow pattern.

When center is reached, pattern is worked exactly in reverse of first side, back to st marker. Pattern will be completed before sts are dec to 40. When completed, fasten off black. Finish slippers in orange.

Cuff: When 40 sts remain, divide them onto double pointed needles. P 1, *k 2, p 2, repeat from * around for 20 (24) rows, depending on length desired. Bind off with number 8 needles or larger.

Finishing Sole: Join an 18 inch piece of yarn at one end of sole opening. Using yarn needle, weave two sides together. Fasten. Clip loose ends.

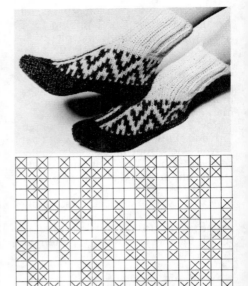

⊠=BLACK ☐=ORANGE

WOMEN'S & CHILDREN'S MITTENS

Challenging

Variegated and solid color yarns are knit alternately to make these warm, attractive mittens. Directions are for women's size with children's size in parentheses. Use about 2 ounces variegated yarn, 2 ounces solid color worsted yarn, 1 set number 4 double pointed needles and 1 set number 6 double pointed needles.

Using smaller needles and solid color, cast on 32 (28) sts. Divide on three needles. Join, being careful not to twist sts.

Work in k 2, p 2 ribbing for 3 inches.

Change to larger needles. K next row, inc one st in every 8th st (7th st)—4 sts inc—36 (32) sts on three needles.

Fasten variegated yarn to solid color, close to needles. K solid color alternately, every other st, with variegated color, inc one st in last st of first row only—37 (33) sts. Continue to alter-

nate solid and variegated yarns for remainder of mitten, thus you will be knitting a solid color on a variegated of previous row and vice versa, except when inc and dec.

K 4 rows.

Next Row: (Start Thumb) K 17 (14) sts, inc one st in next st with same color yarn, inc one st in next st with other color yarn, k next 18 (16) sts—2 sts inc.

Next Row: K around.

Next Row: K 17 (15) sts, inc in next st, k 2, inc in next st, k to end of row—2 sts inc.

Repeat last two rows, inc at both ends of thumb every other row until there are 47 (43) sts on needle—10 sts (8 sts) inc.

Next Row: K around.

Next Row: K 18 (16) sts, place next 10 (8) sts on holder for thumb, k 19 (17) sts—37 (33) sts on needles. K around until piece measures desired length.

Next Row: *K 2 tog, repeat from * around. Join variegated color securely to solid color. Cut off variegated yarn. Cut off solid color yarn, leaving an 8 inch length.

Thread yarn needle, draw yarn through remaining sts. Push to inside of mitten, draw tightly. Weave yarn inside to fasten, cut off excess.

Thumb: Pick up 10 (8) sts for thumb from holder. Divide onto two needles. Pick up 3 more sts on inside of thumb with solid color yarn. K around in solid color on 13 (11) sts for 12 (10) rows or for desired length.

Next Row: (Begin Binding Off) *K 1, k 2 tog, repeat from * around.

Next Row: K around.

Next Row: *K 2 tog, repeat from * around. Fasten off same way as for mitten, drawing yarn to inside and weaving in. Cut off excess.

Repeat directions for second mitten.

Next Row: (Begin Binding Off) *K 1, k 2 tog, repeat from * around.

Next Row: K around.

Next Row: *K 1, k 2 tog, repeat from * around.

FESTIVE BELLS

Easy

Two or three bells in red, green and white make a lovely Christmas corsage or tree decorations. Use pastel shade for baby showers or gold, silver

or white for bridal showers. Materials required for each bell are about 6 yards knitting worsted weight 4-ply yarn, a bead "clapper" for each bell and number 8 standard knitting needles.

Cast on 6 sts.

Row 1: K.

Row 2: Sl st as to k, k 5 (mark sl st end).

Rows 3 through 17: Repeat Rows 1 and 2, end on sl st end. Bind off. DO NOT CUT YARN.

Pick up one st along edge opposite sl sts—19 sts.

Row 1: (Wrong Side) K.

Row 2: P.

Row 3: K.

Bind off in p. Fasten off, leaving about 18 inches yarn. Thread needle and back stitch so seam will not pucker. Pull needle through sl sts and draw together. Fasten securely. Thread bead, measure to bottom of bell. Hold yarns above and below bead together.

through where sl sts are drawn together to right side of bell. Turn bell right side out. Trim end of yarn, tie knot to keep yarn from unwinding.

Tie knot slipping bead through lp and push knot down to bead by pulling yarns in opposite directions. Keeping yarns even, fasten to bell, then pull

---

SNOWMAN FAMILY
Easy

To make this cute boutique snowman family, you need about 4 ounces white, 2 ounces red and 2 ounces green 4-ply yarn, 6 Styrofoam balls, 3 and 4 inches for large snowman, 2½ and 3 inches for medium, 2 and 2½ inches for small, small amounts of black and red felt and number 5 standard knitting needles.

Note: Cut the bottoms of top balls flat as a base. Cut a small amount off top of bottom balls and bottom of top balls. Glue balls together.

MR. SNOWMAN: With white, cast on 30 sts. Work pattern as follows:

Row 1: K.
Row 2: P.

Row 3: P to last 3 sts, turn work.
Row 4: K 27, turn work.
Row 5: K 30.
Rows 6, 7, 8: P.

Repeat Rows 1 through 8 nine times so piece will fit closely over the snowman's head. Bind off. Sew edges together and pull over two Styrofoam balls.

Note: On Row 3, purl to the last 3 stitches and turn, then knit back (which counts as Row 4). On Row 5 knit ALL the way back including the 3 sts not worked on Row 3. This shapes the top of the piece to fit closely around the Styrofoam head. You are not decreasing stitches, but decreasing rows.

Also, the piece does not fit all the way to the top of the head as the hat covers the bare part. For example:

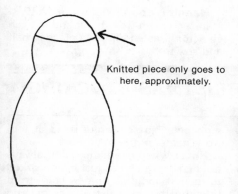

Knitted piece only goes to here, approximately.

Hat: With red, cast on 44 sts. Work 5 rows k 1, p 1 ribbing, then stockinette (k 1 row, p 1 row) until piece measures 2½ inches.

Across next row, k 2 tog, work 3 rows stockinette, one row k 2 tog. Draw up sts. Sew seam. Add pompom.

To Make Pompoms: Wind 20 strands yarn over 2 inch cardboard. Tie around center. Cut ends, trim into ball.

Scarf: With green, cast on 50 sts. Work 4 rows seed st (k the p, p the k sts), bind off. Add tassels.

To Make Tassels: Cut four 4 inch lengths green, pull cut ends through half of the scarf end, tie. Repeat for second half of scarf end. Repeat on opposite end of scarf. Trim evenly.

MRS. SNOWMAN: With white, cast on 22 sts for body. Work Rows 1 through 8 eight times. Finish as with large snowman. On Row 3, k to last 2 sts, turn.

Hat: With red, cast on 34 sts. Work 4 rows ribbing, then stockinette for 2 inches, finish dec and hat as large snowman's hat. Add pompom.

Scarf: With green, cast on 40 sts. Work 2 rows seed st. Bind off. Add tassels, half the size as those of large snowman.

BABY SNOWMAN: With white, cast

on 16 sts. Work Rows 1 through 8 six times. On Row 3, work to last 2 sts, turn. Finish as with large snowman.

Hat: With red, cast on 27 sts. Work 3 rows ribbing, then stockinette to 1¾ inches. Finish dec and hat as for large snowman. Add pompom.

Scarf: With green, cast on 35 sts. Work 2 rows seed st. Bind off. Add tassels.

Add faces to snowpeople with black felt eyes and red felt mouths, in appropriate sizes.

MINIATURE CHRISTMAS STOCKING
Easy

A fun project is this tiny Christmas stocking that can be a placecard, tree ornament or package trim to save from one year to another. Use small amounts of red and white sport weight yarn, standard knitting needles size 2 and crochet hook size E.

Gauge: 8 sts equal 1 inch

With white, cast on 22 sts. Work in garter st (k each row) for 8 rows (4 ridges), fasten off.

Join red and work in stockinette (k 1 row, p 1 row) for 14 rows.

Shape Instep: K 8 and sl to holder,

k 6, sl remaining 8 sts on second holder.

Work center 6 sts (instep) in stockinette for 7 rows, ending with a wrong side row, fasten off. Sl 8 sts from first holder to left hand needle, join red and k these 8 sts, pick up and k 7 sts along side of instep, k across center 6 sts, pick up and k 7 sts along other side of instep, k 8 sts from second holder. P 1 row, k 1 row, p 1 row.

Dec Row: K 2 tog, k 13, k 2 tog, k 2, k 2 tog, k 13, k 2 tog.

P 1 row. Bind off. Sew seams.

Hanging Loop: With white, ch 15, sl st in second ch from hook and in each ch across, fasten off. Fold piece in half and sew to top of stocking.

PEPPERMINT STICK CHRISTMAS STOCKING
Challenging

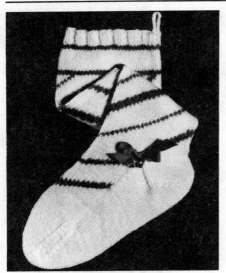

This **Christmas favorite** requires about 4 ounces white, 2 ounces red and a small amount of green knitting worsted weight yarn if personalizing is desired. Use one pair number 5 standard knitting needles and one set number 5 double pointed needles. You also need a crochet hook and bobbins, red ribbon for bow and a small bell.

Gauge: 6 sts equal 1 inch

8 rnds or rows equal 1 inch

With straight needles and white cast on 60 sts. K 2, p 2 in ribbing for 5 rows.

Begin Chart: Following chart, join color indicated and work in stockinette st, changing color where indicated, for 2 rows each of red and white. Draw name desired on large chart, using alphabet chart on white band at top, work name in green.

Note: When changing color, always hold color which has just been worked to the left and pick up new color from underneath. This twists the colors and eliminates a hole. Use separate bobbins for changing each color except when the color is used again after one or two sts of another color.

Work even from chart for 40 rows of chart. Dec one st each end of needle on next row and repeat dec every 8th row 3 times. Work even on 52 sts until 82 rows of chart have been completed. Start instep on last row of chart.

Instep: K 39 sts, sl last 13 sts onto holder (mark last st worked for center of heel). Turn, p 26 sts, sl remaining 13 sts onto another holder (mark last st worked for center of heel). Work chart on 26 sts of instep for 16 rows. Sl these 26 sts onto holder.

Heel: Sl 13 sts of each side of heel from holders onto one double pointed needle, so that marked sts are at center of one needle.

With right side facing, join yarn and work 26 sts in stockinette st for 13 rows.

Next Row: (Turn Heel) P 15, p 2 tog, p 1, turn (leaving remaining sts unworked).

Sl 1, k 5, sl 1, k 1, psso, k 1, turn (leaving remaining sts unworked).

Work from the sts which were left unworked, as necessary, on following rows.

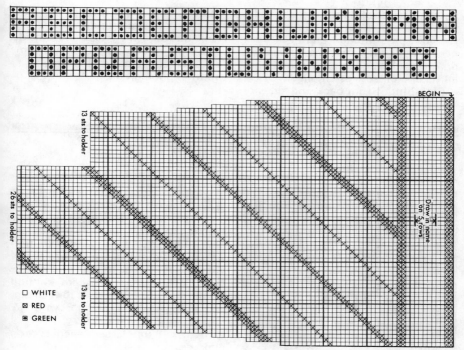

□ WHITE
⊠ RED
⊞ GREEN

Sl 1, p 6, p 2 tog, p 1 from sts which were left unworked, turn.

Sl 1, k 7, sl 1, k 1, psso, k 1 from unworked sts, turn.

Sl 1, p 8, p 2 tog, p 1 from unworked sts, turn.

Continue in this manner, working one st more each time until all unworked sts have been worked, ending with a k row—16 sts remain on needle. Fasten off.

Join yarn at top right side of heel piece and with straight needles pick up and k 12 sts along this side (ends of rows just worked), k each st from 16 st needle, pick up and k 12 sts along the other side of heel piece—40 sts.

Next Row: (Shape Heel Gusset) P.

Next Row: K 1, sl 1, k 1, psso, k to last 3 sts, k 2 tog, k 1.

Repeat last 2 rows until there are 26 sts on needle, ending with a k row.

Foot: Sl last 13 sts just worked onto a double pointed needle (needle 1); with another needle k across instep sts (needle 2); with another needle k remaining 13 sts (needle 3); center of heel is now at beginning of each rnd. K in rnds for 24 rnds and AT SAME TIME continue to work stripes on instep or second needle until there are no red sts left.

Shape Toe: Rnd 1: On needle 1, k to last 3 sts, k 2 tog, k 1; on needle 2, k 1, sl 1, k 1, psso, k to last 3 sts, k 2 tog, k 1; on needle 3, k 1, sl 1, k 1, psso, k to end of rnd.

Rnd 2: K.

Repeat last 2 rnds until there are 16 sts on needles, end with first needle. Sl the 4 sts from needle 3 to needle 1. Leave a 12 inch length for weaving toe, fasten off. Weave toe.

Weaving: Thread yarn in a tapestry needle and hold the two double pointed needles wrong sides together. Weave sts tog as follows: *Pass needle through first st of front needle as if to k and sl st off, pass through 2nd st of front needle as if to p but leave st on needle, draw yarn through, pass needle through first st of back needle as if to p, sl st off, pass through 2nd st of back needle as if to k, leave st on needle, draw yarn through, repeat from * until all sts are joined. Fasten off.

Finishing: Seam back and sides of instep.

Loop: Make a 4 inch chain. Fold chain in half. Starting at ends, weave chain tog for 1 inch. Sew loop inside back seam of stocking. Lightly steam. Sew bow and small bell in place as shown in photograph.

DOLL FACE PILLOW/PAJAMA BAG
Easy

Little people will love this soft cuddly doll, which does double duty as a pajama bag too. Doll pillow requires about 2 ounces each of pale pink, light green and yellow knitting worsted weight yarn. Use small amounts royal blue, brown and red for facial features. Use standard knitting needles numbers 4 and 8, 18 inch zipper, filling material and 1½ yards ¼ inch pink grosgrain ribbon.

BACK: With larger needles and pink, cast on 31 sts (top of head).

Row 1: P.

Row 2: K each st, inc one st at each edge.

Repeat last 2 rows 4 times more—41 sts.

Inc one st each edge every 4th row until there are 53 sts.

P 1 row, k 1 row, p 1 row.

K across, dec one st at each edge.

Continue to dec one st at each edge every 4th row until 41 sts remain.

Dec one st each edge every other row until 31 sts remain, ending with p row.

With smaller needles, k 1, (p 1, k 1), repeat across.

Next 3 Rows: K the k sts, p the p sts as they face you.

Beading Row: *K 1, yo (an inc), k 2 tog (a dec), p 1, repeat from * across, ending last repeat with k 2 tog.

Next Row: Beginning with p 1, work in ribbing. Work 4 more rows in ribbing, fasten off.

With larger needles and blue, inc one st in every third st across—41 sts. In stockinette (k 1 row, p 1 row), work 9

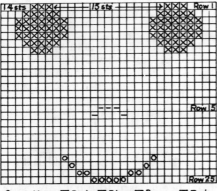

COLOR KEY: □ Pink ☒ Blue ⊟ Brown ◎ Red

rows blue and 10 rows white. With yellow, inc one st in every 4th st across—51 sts. Work 9 rows even.

Repeat white stripe.

Work lavender stripe, inc one st in every fifth st across—61 sts.

Repeat white stripe.

Work pink stripe, inc one st in every 6th st across—71 sts.

Repeat white stripe.

Work green stripe, inc one st in every 7th st across—81 sts.

Bind off sts loosely.

FRONT: Work same as back, until there are 49 sts.

Next Row: P.

Begin Face: (Working from Chart) K 14 sts, k 3 royal blue, k 15, k 3 royal blue, k 14. Continue to work face from chart and complete front same as back.

Finishing: Sew front and back together, leaving cast on sts open at top of head. Block, being careful not to stretch. Make pillow, cutting it ½ inch larger than the head. Lightly stuff with batting. Insert pillow at opening at top of head. Knot 4 strands of yellow fringe in every other cast on st through both front and back side of head, closing the top. Knot fringe on back of head and fold over forehead on front of head. Trim fringe as shown. Hand sew zipper ½ inch to inside around bottom of bag; knot 5 strands of green fringe in every third knit st across lower edges.

Braid: Using yellow, cut 42 strands, each 4 feet long. Divide yarn evenly into three groups and make one braid, braiding tighter at each end so braid looks smaller at ends. Tie each end securely. With yellow, sew braid around face and across fringed area. Trim ends and tie ribbons on each braid. Work ribbon through beading and tie in bow at center front.

Fringe: Wrap yellow around a 12 inch cardboard; cut at both ends. Wrap green yarn around a 10 inch cardboard; cut at both ends.

GOLF CLUB COVERS
Intermediate

Protect your golf clubs with these nifty covers. One ounce knitting worsted weight yarn is sufficient for each cover. Use standard knitting needles numbers 7, 8 and 10.

Sample Swatch: Cast on 14 sts. Work pattern rows.

Pattern Stitch: Row 1: (Right Side) P.

Row 2: P 1, insert needle purlwise in next st and work a long lp st, (to make a long lp st—yarn over loosely around needle twice—an inc made), *p 4, work long lp st in each of next 2 sts, repeat from * across to last 6 sts, p 4, work a long lp st in next st, p 1.

Row 3: K 1, leave yarn on back of work, sl first strand of long lp st as if to p, drop second strand of same long lp st from left needle without working (dec made), *k 4, (sl 1 strand, drop 1 strand) as before in each of next 2 long lp sts, repeat from * across, end k 4, sl 1 strand, drop 1 strand, k 1.

Row 4: P 1, leave yarn at front of work, sl 1 as if to p, *p 4, sl each of next 2 sts as if to p, repeat from * across, end last repeat sl 1, p 1.

Row 5: K 1, sl 1, *k 4, with yarn at back of work, sl 2 as if to p, repeat from * across, end last repeat sl 1 as if to p, k 1.

Row 6: Same as Row 4.

Row 7: K 1, *drop long lp st from needle and leave st on front of work, k 2, pick up long lp st with left needle and k this picked up st, sl 2, drop next lp st, return the 2 slipped sts to left needle, pick up long lp st with left needle and k this picked up st, k each of the 2 slipped sts, repeat from * across, end k 1.

Row 8: K.

Iron Cover: With number 7 needles, cast on 26 sts loosely and work in k 1, p 1 ribbing for 4½ inches. Change to number 8 needles and k across one row, then work pattern st (Rows 1 through 8) 4 times.

Next Row: (Right Side) P.

Next Row: (P 2 sts tog), repeat across —13 sts.

Last Row: K 1, (k 2 sts tog), repeat across, leaving 7 sts.

Cut yarn about 15 inches from work and thread through yarn needle. Sl remaining 7 sts onto cut strand, pull into a closed circle and fasten securely on wrong side, then sew seam on right side, using flat st.

Place dampened club covers over clubs that have been covered with plastic bags. Allow to dry thoroughly.

Wood Cover: Work same as iron cover, using number 8 needles for ribbing and number 10 needles for pattern.

TEAPOT COZY

Intermediate

Tea for two** will be more tempting when the temperature tumbles. Keep your tea hot in this knitted cozy, made in two sections. You will need about 2 ounces of synthetic yarn in knitting worsted weight and small amounts of two contrasting colors. Use numbers 4 and 5 knitting needles and crochet hook size F.

Using smaller needles, cast on 36 sts, work in ribbing of k 1, p 1 for one inch.

Inc Row: Change to larger needles. *K 1, p 1, inc in next k st, p 1, repeat from * across—45 sts. Work in pattern as follows:

Pattern: Row 1: *K 1, p 1, repeat from * across, ending k 1.

Row 2 and All Even Rows: K.

Row 3: K 1, *p 1, k in back of next st, repeat from * across.

Repeat Rows 2 and 3 until there are 10 rows of pattern (5 rows of bumps).

Change to contrasting color and work 6 more rows in pattern, change to second contrasting color and work 2 rows, change to first contrasting color and work 6 rows.

Now change to main color and work 9 rows of pattern.

Dec Row: *K 1, p 1, k 1, p 2 tog, repeat from * across. Work 4 rows in k 1, p 1 ribbing.

Next Row: To make eyelets for drawstring, *k 1, p 1, yo, k 2 tog, repeat from * across.

Work 4 more rows in rib pattern. Work 9 rows in stockinette st (k 1 row, p 1 row). Bind off.

Make second side in same fashion. Sew two sections together leaving opening on sides where contrasting color sections meet. Openings are for spout and handle.

To Make Tie: With two strands of yarn in main color crochet a chain 25 inches long. Thread through holes in 5th row of top ribbing. Make two pompoms by winding yarn around a 1 inch card. Tie to ends of chain.

WOMAN'S KNIT CUFFS

Intermediate

Need new cuffs for a jacket or to make storm sleeves in a coat? Here is the very thing you are looking for. You will need about an ounce of knitting worsted and a set of double pointed knitting needles number 4.

Cast on 44 sts. Divide on 3 needles. Work in k 2, p 2 ribbing for 2½ inches.

Inc to 55 sts by working (k 2, inc 1, p 2) across row.

Work in k 3, p 2 ribbing for 1 inch.

Inc to 66 sts by working (k 2, inc 1, k 1, p 2) across row.

Work in k 4, p 2 ribbing for 1 inch.

Bind off loosely. Sew into coat or on jacket.

MAN'S SKI MASK CAP

Intermediate-Challenging

This cap can be converted to ski mask if desired. It takes about 8 ounces knitting worsted and number 8 standard knitting needles or size needed to obtain gauge.

Gauge: 2 ridges equal 1 inch

Visor: (Underneath Section) Cast on 16 sts.

Row 1: *Yo (an inc), sl 1 as if to p, k 1, repeat from * across—24 sts.

Row 2: Inc one st in first st (to inc: k in front lp of st, leave on needle, k in back of same st, sl st off needle), yo, k the yo of previous row and next st tog (a dec), *yo, sl 1, k the yo and next st tog (a dec), repeat from * across—25 sts.

Row 3: Inc in first st, yo, k 2 tog, *yo, sl 1, k 2 tog, repeat from * across to within last st, inc in last st—27sts.

Row 4: Yo, sl 1, k 1, *yo, sl 1, k 2 tog, repeat from * across, ending inc in last st—29 sts.

Row 5: Yo, sl 1, k 1, *yo, sl 1, k 2 tog, repeat from * across—30 sts.

Repeat Rows 2 through 5 three times —48 sts.

Row 18: *Yo, sl 1, k 2 tog, repeat from * across—48 sts.

Repeat last row until section measures 3½ inches from beginning.

Bind off as follows: K 1, k the yo and next st tog, pass first st over second st, *k 1, bind off, k the yo and next st tog, bind off, repeat from * across.

Outer Section: Cast on 16 sts. Work first 18 rows same as underneath section. Place the 48 sts on stitch holder.

Helmet: Cast on 62 sts.

Work Row 1 same as visor—93 sts.

Repeat Row 18 of visor until section measures 6 inches from beginning.

Next Row: Work in pattern across 24 sts, bind off 45 sts in same way as on visor, work in pattern across last 24 sts.

Next Row: Work in pattern across first group of sts, place the 48 sts from st holder on left needle, yo, sl 1, k 2 tog, continue in pattern across remaining sts. Work in pattern until helmet measures 14½ inches from beginning.

Next Row: *Sl 1, k 2 tog, repeat from * across.

Next Row: P 1, *p 2 tog, p 1, repeat from * across.

Next Row: Sl 1, *k 2 tog, sl 1, repeat from * across.

Next Row: P 2 tog, *p 1, p 2 tog, repeat from * across, fasten off yarn leaving a length for sewing. Pull through all sts, fasten securely.

Finishing: Pin underneath section of visor to outer section. Sew sections together around curved edge. Tack sides and straight edge of underneath section to wrong side of helmet. Weave back seam.

Pompom: Wind yarn 100 times over a 2 inch cardboard. Remove from cardboard. Tie in center, cut both ends and trim. Sew to top of helmet.

WOMAN'S SKI MASK HAT

Intermediate

Keep your face warm in this ski helmet. You will need 4-ply knitting worsted, 3 ounces color A and 2 ounces color B and one set number 9 double pointed needles or size required to obtain gauge.

Gauge: 11 rnds equal 2 inches

Starting at lower edge with A, cast on 88 sts. Divide sts among 3 needles, having 32 sts on first needle and 28 sts on each of 2nd and 3rd needles. Join, being careful not to twist sts.

Rnd 1: *K 2, p 2, repeat from * around.

Repeat first rnd for ribbed pattern. Work in pattern until total length is 10½ inches.

Face Opening: Rnd 1: Bind off in ribbing the 32 sts on first needle. Place A st left on free needle back on 2nd needle. Fasten off A. Join B and complete rnd in ribbing.

Rnd 2: With same strand of B, cast on 32 sts on first needle to replace the 32 bound off sts, complete rnd with B. Continue in rnds of ribbed pattern until B section measures 5 inches.

Top Shaping: Rnd 1: *K 2, p 2, k 2 tog, p 2, repeat from * around—77 sts.

Rnds 2, 3, 4: *K 2, p 2, k 1, p 2, repeat from * around.

Rnd 5: *K 2 tog, p 2, k 1, p 2, repeat from * around—66 sts.

Rnd 6: *K 1, p 2, repeat from * around.

Rnd 7: *K 1, p 2 tog, k 1, p 2, repeat from * around—55 sts.

Rnd 8: *K 1, p 1, k 1, p 2, repeat from * around.

Rnd 9: *K 1, p 1, k 1, p 2 tog, repeat from * around—44 sts.

Rnds 10, 11, 12: *K 1, p 1, repeat from * around.

Rnd 13: *K 1, k 2 tog, p 1, repeat from * around—33 sts.

Rnd 14: *K 2, p 1, repeat from * around.

Rnd 15: *K 2 tog, p 1, repeat from * around—22 sts.

Rnd 16: *K 2 tog, repeat from * around—11 sts.

Fasten off, leaving an 8 inch length of yarn. Thread this yarn into a darning needle and draw through remaining sts; pull up tightly and fasten securely. Press through damp cloth.

THREE-COLOR BELT
Intermediate-Challenging

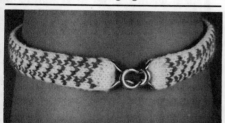

This belt will add a touch of color to your favorite basic dress. Belt requires about one ounce off-white knitting worsted weight yarn and small amounts red and blue. You need one pair number 5 standard knitting needles, any type fastener of correct width and 1 inch elastic the length of belt.

With white, cast on 14 sts.

Row 1: P.

Row 2: K 3, sl 1, k 6, sl 1, k 3.

Repeat Rows 1 and 2 until there are 11 rows.

Joining red and blue and working as before on sts before and after sl sts, begin **pattern on 6 center sts.**

Pattern: Row 1: **On 6 center sts** k 1 blue, k 5 white.

Row 2: P 1 red, p 3 white, p 1 blue, p 1 white.

Row 3: K 2 white, k 1 blue, k 1 white, k 1 red, k 1 white.

Row 4: P 2 white, p 1 red, p 1 white, p 1 blue, p 1 white.

Row 5: K 1 blue, k 3 white, k 1 red, k 1 white.

Repeat Rows 2 through 5 until belt is about 12 rows shorter than desired length, ending after a Row 2. Then work Row 1 once to balance pattern, fasten off red and blue.

Work 11 rows white.

Bind off.

Place elastic on wrong side between sl sts. Fold belt over elastic and sew center seam. Sew on fasteners. Block.

FACIAL TISSUE HOLDER
Easy

Tissues will never get lost or crumpled in this easy-to-make holder. You will need small amounts of colors A and B 3-ply sport yarn. Use knitting needles number 5 and steel crochet hook size 1.

Gauge: 6 sts equal 1 inch

With A, cast on 30 sts, drop A, join B and work as follows:

Row 1: With B, *sl 1 as if to p, k 2, repeat from * across.

Row 2: With B, k.

Row 3: With A, *k 2, sl 1 as if to p, repeat from * across.

Row 4: With A, k.

Repeat these 4 rows until piece measures 6½ inches, end with A, bind off.

With A, work 2 rows sc (ease in slightly) across each end of piece, fasten off.

Fold over each end to meet in center and sew side seams together on inside. Turn piece to right side and steam press.

Special Care For Knitted Articles

After you've spent time and care to complete a knitted piece properly, you don't want to see your work ruined with the first washing. Even if you used the best yarns available improper washing, drying and shaping (called blocking) can leave your piece shrunken, stretched out of shape, or irreparably distorted. Thus it is always good to select better quality yarn for your efforts and pay particular attention to launderability. Before laundering any knitted garment, take the finished measurements so you can block it to the original size after laundering.

LAUNDERING

In some cases the gentle push and pull of laundering can smooth out stitches or rows that were slightly loose or unevenly knitted. To eliminate pulls and ravels, be sure all tail end pieces of yarn are securely woven into the *wrong* side before laundering.

The choice of the proper soap or detergent and method of laundering depends on the fiber content of the yarn. If the yarn is a blend of natural and man-made (synthetic) fibers, always treat it as if it were 100% natural fiber for best results, unless the yarn label says differently. Whenever the yarn label gives laundering instructions, follow them.

NATURAL FIBERS and BLENDS

Turn wrong side out and hand wash with a mild solution of *cold water* soap or detergent product. Care should be taken not to wring, twist or stretch the piece. Rinse thoroughly in cold water, roll in a towel to squeeze out excess water. Smooth out dry towel on a flat surface, gently reshape article on towel as needed and allow to air-dry out of sunlight or direct heat. If pinning is necessary, be sure rustproof pins are used and that no *strain* is put on the yarn. Do not hang to dry and never use bleaches or detergents on wool or wool blends.

SYNTHETIC FIBERS

Turn wrong side out and hand wash or set washing machine for gentle cycle, warm or cold water washing; never hot. Use a mild, cold water detergent or soap product. A fabric softener may be added, but never add bleach. Most synthetics can be machine dried, but if blocking is needed, lay out on a towel on a flat surface. Do not hang to dry and if pinning is needed, use rustproof pins.

BLOCKING

All knitted garments or articles should be blocked in order to have a neat, finished look. A garment may be blocked in separate pieces before joinings are made or after the garment is assembled. To block, lay the knitted piece flat on a padded surface, pin to shape and steam lightly with a warm iron—do not let weight of iron rest on the piece.

Blocking each piece separately: Lay the pieces wrong side up on a flat surface. Shape each piece to the desired measurements and pin with rustproof pins. Lay damp cloth over article and press lightly with a warm iron but do not press hard or allow the iron to rest on the article. A steam iron and pressing cloth may be used. Ribbed cuffs, waistbands and neckbands should never be stretched, only steamed slightly and allowed to dry.

Blocking after finishing: Lay garment flat on a padded surface. Steam out any creases and wrinkles. Pin a one piece dress (for example) across the waistline. Steam one side, allow to dry and then steam the other side.

STIFFENING and SHAPING SPECIAL KNITTED ITEMS

Jewelry items, doilies, dresser scarves and similar show pieces may require stiffening to hold their intricate details in perfect shape. There are several methods that can be used.

For heavy starching, use ½ cup of starch with ½ cup cold water. Stir until completely dissolved, then add 2 quarts of boiling water and cook slowly, stirring constantly, until mixture becomes transparent. Still another thinner starch mixture can be made by dissolving ¼ cup starch in ½ cup cold water. Boil slowly until thick, gradually add 1¼ cups of cold water. Boil, stirring constantly, until starch clears.

Choose and make desired starch solution. Dip knitted item in it and squeeze starch through it thoroughly. Squeeze out excess starch, being sure there is none in open spaces of knitted piece. Stretch and pin piece in true shape on a flat, padded surface; allow to dry thoroughly. Use only rustproof pins.

You may prefer to pin and stretch dampened piece in shape, then brush lightly with liquid plastic starch, being careful not to fill the spaces. Leave to dry thoroughly.

PRESSING

Smooth threads or yarns knitted in flat rows may be pressed by covering with a damp cloth, gently holding a hot iron in place for a few seconds to allow steam from cloth to penetrate piece through cover, lift and move to another place. Never slide iron or hold in one place until cover towel or cloth dries out.

On raised pattern stitches or plushy yarns, either use a damp towel cover and regular iron, or no cover and a steam iron, but in either case *do not* allow iron to touch either cover or item. Iron should be held just above piece and close enough so that steam will thoroughly penetrate item. Remember, synthetics will melt, so *never* let a hot iron touch them under any circumstances!

Garments will retain their shape better if they are folded when not in use. Hanging (especially synthetics) causes stretching out of shape.

Standard Body Measurements

The following body measurements are based on National Knitting Standards. Care should be exercised in using these measurements in knitting for an individual person because nearly everyone varies from the average in one measurement or another. If possible, take all measurements yourself and use this guide to check them or to fill in a measurement you may be lacking. All measurements are in inches unless otherwise indicated. In knitting garments, recheck critical measurements and your gauge of both length and width often to insure a good fit. Take into account whether the garment is to fit loosely or not and whether shrinkage will be a factor.

INFANTS' MEASUREMENTS (allow for growth)

	Small Newborn 5 to 10 lbs.	Medium 6 Month 11 to 18 lbs.	Large 12 Month 19 to 24 lbs.
Chest	to 18″	to 20″	to 22″
Waist	18	19	20
Hip	19	20	21
Back Waist Length	6⅛	6⅞	7½
Across Back	7¼	7¾	8¼
Shoulder	2	2¼	2½
Neck	3¼	3¼	3¼
Sleeve Length to Underarm	6	6½	7½
Armhole Depth	3¼	3½	3¾
Upper Arm Circumference	6½	7	7¼
Wrist Circumference	5	5⅛	5⅛
Head	15	15	16

CHILDREN'S MEASUREMENTS (allow for growth)

	2	3	4	5	6	7	8	10	12	14	16
Chest	21	22	23	24	25	26	27	28½	30	32	33
Waist	20	20½	21	21½	22	22½	23	24	25	25½	26
Hip	22	23	24	25	26	27	28	30	31½	32	33
Back Waist Length	8½	9	9½	10	10½	11½	12½	14	15	15¼	15½
Across Back	8¾	9¼	9½	9¾	10¼	10¾	11	11½	12	12½	13½
Shoulder	2¾	3	3	3⅛	3⅜	3½	3⅝	3¾	4	4½	4¾
Neck	3¼	3¼	3½	3½	3½	3¾	3¾	4	4	4¼	4¼
Sleeve Length to Underarm	8½	9½	10½	11	11½	12	12½	13½	15	15¾	16½
Armhole Depth	4½	4¾	5½	5½	6	6	6¼	6½	7	7¼	7½
Upper Arm Circumference	7½	7¾	8	8¼	8½	8¾	9	9⅜	9¾	9⅞	10
Wrist Circumference	5¼	5¼	5½	5½	5½	5¾	5¾	6	6	6⅛	6⅛

Note: At Size 14 girls may switch to "misses" and at size 16 boys may switch to "men's" sizes.

MISSES' MEASUREMENTS

	6	8	10	12	14	16	18
Bust	30½	31½	32½	34	36	38	40
Waist	23	24	25	26½	28	30	32
Hip	32½	33½	34½	36	38	40	42
Back Waist Length	15½	15¾	16	16¼	16½	16¾	17
Across Back	13½	13½	14	14½	15	15½	16
Shoulder	4¾	4¾	5	5	5	5¼	5¼
Neck	4	4	4	4½	5	5	5½
Sleeve Length to Underarm	16¾	16¾	17	17½	17¾	18	18¼
Armhole Depth	7	7	7½	7½	7½	8	8
Upper Arm Circumference	9¾	9¾	10¼	10½	11	11½	12
Wrist Circumference	6	6	6¼	6¼	6½	6½	6½

WOMEN'S MEASUREMENTS

	38	40	42	44	46	48	50
Bust	42	44	46	48	50	52	54
Waist	35	37	39	41½	44	46½	49
Hip	44	46	48	50	52	54	56
Back Waist Length	17¼	17⅜	17½	17⅜	17¾	17⅞	18
Across Back	16½	17	17½	18	18	18½	18½
Shoulder	5½	5½	5¾	5¾	6	6¼	6¼
Neck	5½	6	6	6	6	6	6
Sleeve Length to Underarm	18¼	18¼	18¼	18¼	18¼	18¼	18¼
Armhole Depth	8¼	8¼	8¼	8½	8½	8¾	8¾
Upper Arm Circumference	13	13½	14	15	15¾	16½	17
Wrist Circumference	6¾	7	7¼	7½	7¾	8	8

MEN'S MEASUREMENTS

	34	36	38	40	42	44	46	48
Chest	34	36	38	40	42	44	46	48
Waist	28	30	32	34	36	39	42	44
Hip	35	37	39	41	43	45	47	49
Across Back	15½	16	16½	17	17½	18	18½	19
Shoulder	5	5¼	5½	5½	5½	6	6	6
Neck: shirt size	14	14½	15	15½	16	16½	17	17
Length to Armhole	14	14½	15	15½	16	16	16½	17
Armhole Depth	8	8½	9	9½	10	10½	11	11½
Sleeve to Underarm	17½	18	18½	19	19½	20	20	20½
Back Length	22	23	24	25	26	26½	27½	28½

Common Metric Equivalents

Metric measurements are being used more and more in American knitting pattern instructions.

The following chart lists measurements most commonly used in knitting and their metric equivalents. Note that these metric units are given in *millimeters* (mm), thousandths of a meter; or in *centimeters* (cm), hundredths of a meter. A meter measures 39.37 inches, or 3.37 inches longer than our yard.

Inches	(mm's) Millimeters
⅛	3
¼	6
½	13
¾	20
1¼	32
1½	38
1¾	44
2	51
2½	63
3	76
3½	90

Inches	(cm's) Centimeters
4	10
4¼	11
5	13
5½	14
6	15
6⅝	17
7	18
7⅜	19
7¾	20
8¼	21
9	23
9⅜	24
10⅛	26
11	28
11¾	30
12¼	31
13	33
13¾	35
14¼	36
15	38
15¾	40
16½	42
17	43
17¾	45
18½	47
19¼	49
20	51
21¼	54
22	56
23¼	59
24¾	63
25½	65
27½	70
29¼	74
31½	80
33	84
35	89

Notes